Anarchy

Praise for Dave Andrews

One of the leading prophetic voices of our times.
Mike Riddell, *Godzone*

Writes with a wealth of experience on matters dear to my heart.
Jim Wallis, *Sojourners*

A deep thinker who has a rare gift of interpreting the activities and motivations of [the] society where he finds himself.
Mike Feeron, *Christian Week*

He is offering more than a practical sound bite. With Dave Andrews, theory has become practice, and truths take on a life of their own.
Simon Mayo, BBC Radio 1

This English-born Australian-sounding father of two is really a kind of urban peace guerrilla!
Clive Price, *Christian Family*

Dave is ordinary, but believes ordinary people should take extraordinary risks to confront the cruelty in our world!
David Engwicht, *Eco-City*

People like Dave could be branded 'radical' and be shunned ... But he does not harangue people. He provides [us] with suggestions to help us look at our communities.
Irene Oliver, *Queensland Baptist*

Dave has a calmness that radiates serenity [and] a warm human understanding.
Ranjan Gupta, *Sydney Morning Herald*

Very practical, compassionate, and empowering.
Trevor Jordan, *Dayspring*

Dave Andrews has long excited our admiration for his work with marginalised people. Dave makes us ask [ourselves] if we can build a better world. If there were more people like Dave, and his partner Ange, to inspire us, we would be able to reply with a resounding 'Yes!'
Charles Elliott, *Signs of our Times*

Praise for *Christi-Anarchy*

This is a courageous and provocative study, likely to earn applause from some, and brickbats from others, but certain to challenge and to stimulate serious reflection.

Dave Andrews attacks Christian complacency and calls us back to the non-violent, yet radically subversive 'Way' of Jesus.

Many of us who teach church history feel uncomfortable with facile explanations of its dark, demonic side.

This book confronts that darkness with a sobering accusation: post-Constantinian Christianity has so perverted the 'Way' that, far from being aberrations, atrocities have become its natural excrescences.

Christianity's reputation is so besmirched that a startling, new name is proposed for the humble, loving 'Way' of life taught and exemplified by Jesus.

Those afraid of moving out of their comfort zone are advised not to read this book!

Professor Patricia Harrison, PhD, Tabor College, Sydney, Australia

The long history of the project Christendom may be typified as the house of authority, with its many attendant abuses of power. But a different thread runs through history as well, based on the subversive memory of the early Jesus movement. This could be typified as the house of freedom.

Here welcome, hospitality, downward mobility, servant leadership, common purse, intentional community, peace and justice are the dancing residents.

In the tradition of Vernard Eller, Dave Andrews invites us to dwell in the house of freedom, and fling open all the doors and windows!

Professor Charles Ringma, PhD, Regent College, Vancouver, Canada

This book is a radical but loving reconstruction of the movement of Jesus Christ, in protest against its distortions.

Dave Andrews, one of the leading prophetic voices of our time, brings all of his passion and insight to bear in a way which will both disturb and inspire.

Christi-Anarchy has that uncomfortable air of a message crying out ot be heard, and I hope it is widely read.

Mike Riddell, author of *alt.spirit@metro.m3* and *Godzone*

Christi-Anarchy

Discovering
a radical spirituality
of compassion

Dave Andrews

WIPF & STOCK · Eugene, Oregon

Wipf and Stock Publishers
199 W 8th Ave, Suite 3
Eugene, OR 97401

Christi-Anarchy
Discovering a Radical Spirituality of Compassion
By Andrews, Dave and Costello, Tim
Copyright©1999 by Andrews, Dave
ISBN 13: 978-1-61097-852-1
Publication date 2/1/2012
Previously published by Tafina Press, 1999

Introduction to Dave Andrews for the 2012 Dave Andrews Legacy Series

I KEPT seeing this guy on the shuttle bus - long hair, graying beard, a gentle 60's-70's feel to him. He seemed thoughtful, intense, friendly, and quiet, like he had a lot on his mind, as did I. Even though I saw him nearly every time I boarded the shuttle bus, we didn't speak beyond him smiling and saying, "G'day" and me nodding and saying, "Hey" as we boarded or disembarked.

It was my first time at Greenbelt, a huge festival about faith, art, and justice held every August in the UK. I had always heard great things about the event and so was thrilled when I was invited to speak. I was just as thrilled to get a chance to hear in person some musicians and speakers I had only heard about from a distance, so I went through the program and marked people I wanted to be sure not to miss.

It was near the end of the conference when a friend told me to be sure to catch an Australian fellow named Dave Andrews. "I've never heard of him," I said. "Oh, he's a force of nature," my friend said. "Kind of like Jim Wallis, Tony Campolo, and Mother Teresa rolled up into one." How could I not put a combination like that in one of the last free slots on my schedule?

I arrived at the venue a few minutes late and there he was, the bearded guy from the bus. Thoughtful, intense, and friendly, yes - but *quiet* he was not. He was nearly exploding with passion - passion and compassion, in a voice that ranged from fortissimo to fortississimo to furioso. How could a guy churning with so much hope, love, anger, energy, faith, fury, and curiosity have been so quiet and unassuming on the bus?

He was a force of nature indeed, evoking from his audience laughter, shouts, amens, reverent silence, and even tears before he was done. He spoke of justice, of poverty, of oppression, of solidarity across religious differences, of service, of hope, of celebration, of the way of Jesus.

As I listened, I wanted to kick myself. *This is the most inspiring talk I've heard at this whole festival. Why did I miss all those opportunities to get to know this fellow on the bus? Now the festival is almost over and I've missed my chance!*

Later than evening, I boarded the shuttle bus for the last ride back to my hotel, and there sat Dave and his wife, Ange. I didn't miss my chance this time. I introduced myself and they reciprocated warmly.

I was a largely unknown American author at the time and hardly known at Greenbelt, much less in Australia, so I'm quite certain Dave and Ange had never heard of me. But they couldn't have been kinder, and as we disembarked, he pulled two books from his backpack and told me they were a gift.

The next day when I flew home from Heathrow, I devoured them both on the plane. First, I opened *Not Religion, But Love* and read it through from cover to cover. Then I opened *Christi-anarchy* and couldn't put it down either. When my plane landed, I felt I had been on a spiritual retreat . . . or maybe better said, in a kind of spiritual boot camp!

Things I was thinking but had been afraid to say out loud Dave was saying boldly and confidently. Ideas I was very tentatively considering he had already been living with for years. Complaints and concerns I only shared in highly guarded situations he was publishing from the housetops. Hopes and ideals I didn't dare to express he celebrated without embarrassment.

iv

I think I gave him a copy of one or two of my books as well, and I guess he was favorably impressed enough that we stayed in touch and a friendship developed. I discovered that we were both songwriters as well as writers, that we both had a deep interest in interfaith friendships, that we both had some critics and we both had known the pain of labeling and rejection.

Since then, whatever he has written, I've been sure to read . . . knowing that he speaks to my soul in a way that nobody else does.

We've managed to get together several times since our initial meeting in England, in spite of the fact that we live on opposite sides of the planet. We've spoken together at a few conferences on both hemispheres, and I had the privilege of visiting him in Brisbane. I've seen the beautiful things he has been doing in a particularly interesting and challenging neighborhood there, walking the streets with him, meeting his friends, sensing his love for that place and those people. He's been in my home in the US as well, and we've been conspiring for some other chances to be and work together in the future.

In my speaking across North America, I frequently refer to Dave's work, but until now, his books have been hard to come by. That's why I'm thrilled to introduce this volume to everyone I can in North America.

Yes, you'll find he's one part Tony Campolo, one part Jim Wallis, and one part Mother Teresa, a force of nature, as I was told.

You'll also find he is a serious student of the Bible and a serious theological sage — the kind of reflective activist or thinker-practitioner that we need more of.

In a book like *Christi-anarchy*, he can boldly and provocatively unsettle you and challenge you. Then in a book like *Plan Be*, he can gently and pastorally encourage and inspire you. Like the central inspiration of his life, he is the kind of person to confidently turn over tables in the Temple one minute and then humbly defend a shamed and abused woman from her accusers the next.

You'll see in Dave's writings that he is highly knowledgeable about poverty, ecology, psychology, sociology, politics, and economics . . . not only from an academic standpoint, but also from a grassroots, experiential level. His writing on these subjects grows from what he has done on the ground . . . for example, nurturing a community network that is training young adults to live and serve among the poor, supervising homes for adults who are learning to live with physical and psychiatric disabilities, encouraging small businesses to hire people who others would consider unemployable and developing a non-profit solar energy co-op for local people.

Dave's writings and friendship have meant so much to me. I consider him a friend and mentor. Now I am so happy that people across North America can discover him too.

You'll feel as I did — so grateful that you didn't miss the chance to learn from this one-of-a-kind, un-categorizable, un-containable, wild wonder from Down Under named Dave Andrews.

Brian D. McLaren
author/speaker/activist (brianmclaren.net)

Foreword

This book begins with the painful experience of Dave Andrews being ousted from a Christian community, and ends with the beautiful outworking of community inspired by the example of the Christ who continues to inspire Dave, and his partner, Ange.

It is a passionate journey.

These pages reveal a genuine ongoing struggle with the chequered history of Christianity—and its often over-powering institutions and spirit-deadening ideas—as Dave seeks to re-think what it means to be a follower of Jesus.

Dave's conclusions are not mere statements. I've discovered over many years Dave's words reflect his actions, and his actions are fleshed out in the community where he now works. *Christi-Anarchy* has the potential to change the outworking of faith, and the very fabric of society. It is a vision that can transform individualistic self-serving localities into whole-hearted communities.

Reverend Tim Costello
Melbourne, Australia, 1999

For
my brothers and my sisters,
my in-laws and out-laws

Acknowledgments

I would like to thank Ange, Marty and Evonne, Phil and Karen, Ruth, and Mary for reading the text at an early stage, and giving me their encouragement to continue with the project.

I would also like to thank John Rees for his critique of the content; Mike Riddell for his suggestions about the style; and Manu Caddie for his ideas about graphics and design.

My thanks to Tim Costello for writing the original foreword; Roland at Tafina Press for taking the risk to re-publish this book; and Maurice Lyon for doing the work that was required to make the book as readable as it is.

I'd also like to thank *Dayspring, Transformation*, and *On Being* for being able to use excerpts from articles I wrote that were originally published in their magazines.

And I'd particularly like to thank my friends in Dilaram, Aashiana and The Waiters' Union who helped me discover Christi-Anarchy.

Contents

Preface to the Tafina edition

When *Christi-Anarchy* was first published it caused quite a bit of controversy. Some claimed it was 'a denial of two thousand years of Christian tradition'!

At one time Koorong, the biggest Christian booksellers in Australia, refused to stock *Christi-Anarchy* openly on their shelves lest it 'cause offence' to their customers. Patricia Harrison, of Tabor College Sydney, warned readers: 'Those afraid of moving out of their comfort zone are advised *not* to read this book.'

But in spite of the controversy that surrounded its publication *Christi-Anarchy* has become a bit of a cult classic – or should I say, 'occult classic'.

Believe it or not, *Christi-Anarchy* has been displayed as best seller in the Occult Section of Avid Books, a local West End book store, whose manager reported that it was so popular that people were stealing it off the shelves! Christians report 'non-Christian' friends sending them copies of the book by post with a note suggesting that, after they read it, they meet to talk about it.

I wasn't surprised the book was received well by people who were disillusioned with Christianity, and who used the book as a conversation starter to talk with Christian friends about their disillusionment. But I was surprised that so many nice, straight, middle-class, middle-of-the-road, evangelical and charismatic Christians responded to the book so appreciatively.

I will never forget the phone call I got from my elder sister Ruth, who was an Australian Baptist missionary in Thailand. I'd sent her a copy of the book and I'd waited rather anxiously for her reply, as I was uncertain how she would take it. When Ruth eventually called me, all she could do was cry, and say over and over again: 'Thanks for writing *Christi-Anarchy*, Dave. It says what I think but what I've never had the words—or the courage—to say publicly myself.' It was a sentiment that I was to hear expressed repeatedly wherever I went. But I must confess, I never expected to hear it from my friends in YWAM.

However last year, when I was visiting some YWAM friends in the US, they not only affirmed what I was saying; they actually asked my permission to publish what I was saying in the *International YWAMer*. So in January 2004, against all the odds, YWAM published an interview with me entitled 'Leaving Room for Doubt'—recommending YWAMers buy copies of *Christi-Anarchy*!

Patricia Harrison says that *Christi-Anarchy* is 'a courageous and provocative study, likely to earn applause from some, and brickbats from others, but certain to challenge and to stimulate serious reflection.' I hope so.

Dave Andrews, Brisbane 2004

Preface

Our planet is in trouble.

Religion, which was meant to make things better, often has made things worse—far, far worse. Christianity, the dominant religion in the world today, has been charged with utter disregard for human rights, proven guilty of total destruction of tribal cultures, and implicated in some of the worst cases of genocide in the twentieth century.

Recently, I was called in to discuss these matters with a committee appointed by the synod of a church in my own home state. I was greeted at the door, and shown a chair at the end of a table, around which were seated a set of some of the most seriously dressed men I had ever seen.

When we were all seated, a very sombre-looking man, at the head of the table, announced that he would select a passage from the Bible to set the scene for our discussion. He picked up the big old book on the table in front of him, and, in a deep stentorian voice, began to read:

'In the cities of the nations, the Lord your God is giving you as an inheritance: Do not leave anything that breathes alive! Completely destroy them—the Hittites, the Amorites, the Canaanites, the Perizzites, the Hivites and the Jebusites—as the Lord your God has commanded you!' (Deuteronomy 20:16-17)

Then, the Sombre Man closed the book ,and said, 'So you can see, in the Bible there is no such thing as "inalienable human rights". God's people are simply called to do God's will,' he said, with a cold, hard, matter-of-fact finality, 'whether that is to cure, or to kill!'

I could hardly believe my ears. Here I was, in downtown Brisbane, the capital of peaceful sunny Queensland—'beautiful one day, perfect the next'—and I was listening to a Christian leader justifying wholesale slaughter in the name of God!

This book explores the incredible, callous disregard for the rights of others that is so typical of Christianity, and seeks to answer the question: is it possible to rehabilitate Christianity as a religion, or not?

If you have ever been drawn to the person of Christ, but had real reservations about the Christianity you have encountered as a religion, then this book is for you.

Dave Andrews, Brisbane 1999

Memo To J.C.

When you was down here J.C.,
You were a pretty decent sort of bloke.
Although you never owned nothing
But the clothes on your back,
And you were always walking around, broke.
You'd talk to people and you didn't judge,
You didn't mind helping the down and out.
But these fellows preaching now in your name,
Just what are they on about?
Didn't you tell these fellows to do other things
Besides all that preaching and praying?
Well listen J.C. there's things ought to be said,
And I might as well get on with saying,
Didn't you tell them 'don't judge', 'love one another',
And 'not to put your faith in worldly goods'?
Well: you should see the goods they got, brother!
They got great big buildings and works of art
And millions of dollars of real estate!
They got no time to care about human beings;
They even forgot what they told you 'em mate:
Things like 'whatever you do to the least of these
you do it also unto me.'
Yeah, well these people who are using your good name,
They're abusing it, J.C.!

But there's people still living the way you lived.
And still copping the hypocrisy and hate.
Getting crucified by the fat cats, too.
But they don't call us religious, mate.
Tho' we got the same basic values that you lived by—
Sharin' and carin' about each other.
And the bread and the wine that you passed around—
Well, we're still doing that, brother.
Yeah, we share our food and drink and shelter,
Our grief, our happiness, our hopes, and plans -
But they don't call us 'Followers of Jesus';
They call us 'Black Fellas', man.
But if you're still offering your hand in forgiveness,
To the sinner who says he's sorry,
I reckon we'll meet up later on,
And I got no cause to worry.
Just don't seem right that all the good you done
That people preach, not practise, what you said.
I wonder, if it all died with you, that day on the cross
And if it just never got raised from the dead?

Maureen Watson, Australian aboriginal poet

Prologue

Why? - Wham!

There's nothing quite like getting hit over the head to make you think about things a bit more. My moment of awakening came when I got mugged by YWAM.

For the uninitiated, YWAM, pronounced '*Why? - Wham!*', stands for Youth With A Mission, which with its vast army of thousands of gung-ho, voluntary, young evangelists, is not only one of the biggest, but also one of the most energetic (and some would say, most aggressive) mission agencies in the world today. For me, getting done over by YWAM was a bit like being a dummy getting pummelled to death by the troops during training at boot camp. Needless to say, it was a salutary way for me to learn not to be such a dummy in future.

We first encountered YWAM when my wife Ange and I, along with a whole generation of flower-power Jesus freaks, had been checking out alternative communities, and had come across this up-and-coming group a lot of people were talking about, called Youth With A Mission.

Now YWAM is nothing if not amazing, and at its best it can bedazzle the best of us. It always has been, and still is, a very impressive movement.

YWAM has over 2,000 workers in more than forty countries, with its own private university, The University of the Nations, to train its personnel, and its own private fleet of ships known as 'The Mercy Ships', to take YWAMers on errands of mercy, 'delivering relief supplies, construction materials, and medical services to needy islands', while they 'sail the clear blue waters of the South Pacific.'

Now you've got to admit, that sounds pretty good, doesn't it? But right from the start, Ange and I knew YWAM was not for us. We found YWAM an extra-ordinary, larger-than-life, high-flying, fast-moving, do-anything, go-anywhere, global evangelistic agency. What Ange and I were really looking for, was a more-ordinary, small-is-beautiful, low-profile, long-term, hands-on, grass-roots, local community ministry.

Ironically enough, though we didn't find what we were looking for in YWAM, we did find what we were looking for through YWAM. Because through YWAM, Ange and I met an ex-YWAMer with the unlikely name of Floyd McClung Jr., and it was courtesy of this lovable, lanky, long-haired, full-bearded, 6' 7", gentle giant, that we were introduced to a community called 'Dilaram: The House of the Peaceful Heart', that was to become our home.

Our next memorable encounter was when YWAM, believe it or not, was proposing a 'marriage' to us of some sort! Our time in Dilaram had been a dream come true. For in the House of the Peaceful Heart, Ange and I had seen a vision for society, that our generation held dear, become a reality. A partial reality? Certainly. An ephemeral reality? Apparently. But it was a beautiful reality nonetheless. It was the experience of people simply just being able to live together in peaceful, compassionate, therapeutic communities. When word got out about it, crowds of young people from all over the world made their way to join us in our quiet little revolution.

So the movement began to gather some momentum. Floyd and Sally set up the first Dilaram Community in Kabul, Afghanistan. Then Harry and Rosie started the second Dilaram Community in Kathmandu, Nepal, and Ange and I started the third Dilaram

Community in Delhi, India with Steve and Kathy Aram. We got on a bit of a roll, and it only took a few years for us to establish a dozen different Dilaram Communities in half a dozen different countries around the world. During this time, YWAM had offered Dilaram the use of some houseboats in Amsterdam to establish a community in the Netherlands.

Loren Cunningham, the Director of YWAM, had used the opportunity this cooperative venture presented, to resolve a conflict that he'd had with Floyd that had caused Floyd to leave YWAM. But as time went by, it became clear that Loren Cunningham had much more on his mind than conflict resolution. Loren was so impressed with the job Floyd had done with Dilaram, that he not only wanted Floyd to come back to YWAM, but he also wanted Floyd to come back and take over his role as the Director of YWAM! Knowing Floyd as well as he did, it wasn't difficult for Loren to make him an offer he knew he couldn't refuse.

And as for Dilaram—'Well . . . what about a merger? Couldn't there be a merger between YWAM and Dilaram? It would be kinda like—a marriage. A marriage. That's it! Now, tell me, what could be nicer than that?'

Without doubt our most memorable encounter with YWAM was when they excommunicated me, pitched me and my family out of our home, dumped us in the street, and banned everybody, on pain of excommunication, from helping us.

As you can imagine, I have often asked myself what I did to make them so mad at me.

Right from the start, from the very moment when the idea of a merger between YWAM and Dilaram was mooted, I had some very serious reservations about it. Ange and I, like many others, had joined Dilaram rather than YWAM because we wanted to be a part of Dilaram, not a part of YWAM. We feared that if we entered into this so-called 'marriage', given what appeared to us to be a very patriarchal approach, Dilaram would inevitably be expected to play a subordinate role to YWAM. And we were scared that, in the process of that subordination, the very identity of Dilaram as a movement would be subsumed into the hegemony of YWAM as an organisation, like a cluster of little folksy corner stores being absorbed into a big multinational brandname chain.

Even before any official takeover had taken place, we had begun to notice worrying signs that indicated that the YWAMisation of Dilaram was well under way. People were beginning to be expected to go through a YWAM orientation course before being allowed to join a Dilaram Community. Not only were Dilaram leaders being expected to attend YWAM leaders' conferences, but Dilaram leaders were also being expected to lead their communities in the more directive YWAM style that was modelled at those conferences. And the incentives for Dilaram leaders to take on the YWAM style were really attractive: a higher position, a wider reputation, greater privileges, and bigger perks—called 'love gifts'. I became increasingly concerned about these trends, because I was convinced that if we succumbed to these temptations, then sooner or later, quarrels about power would inevitably destroy the very spirit of liberty and equality in our communities that I loved. So I decided to speak out against the YWAMisation of Dilaram.

Little did I know, that even then it was already too late. When I did speak out, I assumed that the Dilaram ethos still prevailed, and that people could still speak out openly about an issue, and take opposing sides in a dispute, with the expectation that in the end, we would all be able to sit down together and settle the matter amicably.

However, this assumption was to prove to be false. At one stage, in the middle of the debate about the future of Dilaram, I was sent to consult with some of the other communities. While I was away, who should turn up at my community, but Loren Cunningham, the Director of YWAM himself. In my absence, Loren did his best to portray my criticism of Floyd's position on the YWAMisation of Dilaram, as nothing but a devious, underhanded attempt to undermine Floyd's leadership. Before he left, Loren melodramatically made it a point to pronounce woe upon those who would dare to touch the Lord's anointed.

Now I don't know a lot about 'woes'. But I can tell you that the particular woe Loren had in mind for me, wasn't the kind of woe I had to wonder about, before it hit me like a hammer.

Floyd called me and told me that, on my return, it probably would be better if I did not come back to the community, but meet him at the airport. When I eventually arrived at the airport I was met, not only by Floyd, but also by the International Council of YWAM, who had flown in from the four corners of the compass to help Floyd deal with me.

It was a set up. An ambush. I was completely taken by surprise. And before I had the chance to recover my wits well enough to defend myself, the International Council of YWAM proceeded to take me apart. They said I was a rebel, and, as an unrepentant rebel, would be summarily excommunicated.

I said that they misunderstood me: that I opposed the YWAM takeover of Dilaram that Floyd had proposed, but I had never intended to oppose Floyd himself. They said they understood me better than I understood myself: that in the very process of disputing the YWAM takeover of Dilaram that Floyd supported, I had already positioned myself, in policy terms, to displace Floyd himself.

I said that was nonsense. The whole point of my protest was to affirm the importance of bottom-up leadership and to confront the development of top-down leadership. Given that perspective, I said, it would make no sense for me to put myself in a position I disputed. But they wouldn't listen.

Look, I said, to prove to you that I have absolutely no interest at all in expanding my power base in Dilaram, especially at my friend Floyd's expense, I would be more than willing to take a vow of silence for the next six months—during which time I would take on the job of cleaning the toilets in any Dilaram Community you want to choose—on condition that at the end of the six months you bring me before an assembly of Dilaram Communities, you can state your view, I can state mine, and we can allow the assembly to settle this matter once and for all.

They sat there for a while. Saying nothing. Then they said something I will never forget. They said, it didn't matter what I said, there would be no deal. Because the Lord had shown them that I was a rebel and they couldn't risk my being brought before a meeting of my peers lest I incite them to rebellion too. The only thing, they said, the Lord would have them do, with a rebel like me, was to excommunicate me.

So they did. Right there, right then. In the restaurant at the airport.

From that moment on, I was no longer allowed to be part of the community that, up until then, had been my whole life. I was literally put out of my home. And not permitted to return.

Not even to pick up my luggage. Lest anyone talk to me. And, of course, everyone was forbidden to talk with me or offer me any help at all. Those who did so risked the same treatment themselves. So few did.

In the ensuing days I tried to talk with people. But even people, who had been my friends, who saw me coming down the street towards them, would turn their back on me and walk away. Dr Ray Windsor, the Director of Interserve, one of the most well respected mission agencies in the world, tried to intervene, and speak on my behalf, but he got no better hearing than I did.

I was devastated that people I respected wouldn't even give me the time of day, but would precipitously pitch me and my family out of our home, dump us out in the street, and then ban everybody, on pain of excommunication, from helping us, all in the name of the Lord.

Now, as I said, there's nothing quite like getting hit over the head to make you think about things a bit more. And, as I thought about things, I desperately tried to make some sense of the tragic sequence of events that had turned my greatest dream into my worst nightmare, and had reduced me to complete and utter despair.

To start with I thought about the part that I had played in the catastrophe myself. At the time I couldn't recollect anything that I'd done wrong. I could only remember the things that I'd done right. I'd stood by my commitment to my community, and consequently taken a strong stand against a corporate takeover that threatened to destroy that community. I'd listened to a lot of little people who were being hurt in the process. And I'd spoken up, on their behalf, to the big people, who were trampling their feelings underfoot. I'd resisted the inducements that were secretly offered to me in a bid to buy me off. And I'd fought a gallant fight in a losing battle for the sake of the liberty and the equality that I believed in.

However, in hindsight, some of my 'heroic' actions were rather less than that. No doubt my words and my deeds were well intentioned, but I think that in the heat of the debate, when my blood was up, many of the things I said and did must have been very insensitive, and unnecessarily hurtful. Over time I have come to understand that the insensitivity that I displayed in that situation was no accident, but the inevitable outcome of my tendency to be preoccupied with ideology, just holding the line, rather than with

7

love, which can extend kindness, while holding a line, to both friend and foe alike.

Therefore, although it was never my intention to cause Floyd any grief, to be fair to Loren, I must confess that coming to blows with Floyd over the future of Dilaram in the way I did, made it easy for someone like him, who didn't really know me, to think that it was so.

Having thought about the part I had played in the debacle, I then thought about the part other people had played in my demise. Most of what I thought about others is not a matter for public discussion, but a matter for private conversation between them and me, that I have taken up at every appropriate opportunity.

Suffice it to say that I know Floyd was terribly embarrassed about the whole affair and he has made it a matter of public record that he wishes he had not acted the way he did. But the question of why YWAM acted the way they did, needs to be answered. At one level, that can be answered in personal terms. Loren wanted Floyd as his successor and, as a man of faith, he was prepared to move heaven and earth to get what he wanted. And Floyd was more than willing to go along with what Loren wanted because, by becoming the Director of YWAM, he could become one of the most significant mission leaders in modern times.

At another level, the question of why YWAM acted the way they did, can be answered in organizational terms. YWAM needed more energetic leadership. And Floyd undoubtedly fitted the bill: as fine a capable young charismatic leader as you could find.

Maybe YWAM wanted Dilaram. Maybe YWAM just wanted Floyd. I don't know. But, if Dilaram was what it took to get Floyd, it seemed like YWAM was determined to take it over, come hell or high water. So when I stood like King Canute, trying to stop the

YWAM tide from taking over Dilaram, I was doomed from the start. YWAM didn't really have anything against me as a person. YWAM as an organisation, simply swept me out of their way in pursuit of their corporate plans.

At yet another level, the question of why YWAM acted the way they did, can be answered in theological terms. In fact, it was in these terms that YWAM themselves chose to justify their actions. When people questioned YWAM, as to why they did what they did, the answer was always "It was the Lord that told them." It was the Lord that had told them that I was a rebel. It was the Lord that had told them that they couldn't risk me, as a rebel, being brought before a meeting of my peers, lest I incite them to rebellion too. It was the Lord that had told them that the only thing they could do, with an unrepentant rebel like me, was to excommunicate me.

It was the Lord that had told them that from that moment on, I should no longer be allowed to be part of the community that, up until then, had been my whole life. It was the Lord that had told them that I ought to be put out of my home, and not permitted to return, not even to pick up my luggage, because it was imperative that nobody relate to me at all. Finally, it was the Lord that had told them that anybody who helped a rebel like me should be treated like a rebel themselves, and be summarily excommunicated.

So the greatest injustice that I had ever experienced in my life, was justified in the name of Christ.

Christl-Anarchy

A History of Christianity: a History of Cruelty

I was brought up to believe that the history of Christianity was a history of Christlike spirituality, that shone through the centuries like a light in the darkness. But I've come to realise that Christianity itself has a dark side, and that the history of Christianity is as much a litany of cruelty as it is a legacy of charity.[1]

Councils, creeds, and coercion: ca. AD 100 – 500

Christianity may have begun as a voluntary nonviolent movement committed to authentic human growth and change. But it wasn't long before it became a fierce reactionary force, which fervently circumscribed personal choice and ferociously suppressed political dissent.

It was during the reign of the Emperor Constantine that Christianity in the Roman Empire started to align itself with the established order. Constantine saw the religion as a means of uniting a fragmented empire, and the church saw the state as a means of securing a favoured position for its religion.

So the deal was done: in return for encouraging the people to obey the authorities, pay taxes, and serve in the army, the clergy were exempt from being tried by secular courts,[2] paying customary taxes,[3] and serving in the regular army themselves.[4] In return for the sign of the cross, and the assurance that 'in this sign thou shalt conquer', the Emperor Constantine at the Council of Nicea in 325, ensured unanimous acceptance of the Nicene Creed as the standard of orthodoxy, by threatening to banish any bishop who disagreed.[5]

During the reigns of the Emperors Theodosius and Honorius that followed, Christianity in general, and the Catholic Church in particular, managed to become synonymous with the status quo itself. In 380 Emperor Theodosius passed a decree that stated:

> We shall believe in the single Deity ... of the Holy Trinity. We command that those persons who follow this rule shall embrace the name of Catholic Christians. The rest, however, ... who shall sustain the infamy of heretical dogmas, ... whom we adjudge demented and insane, shall be smitten first by divine vengeance, and secondly by retribution of our own initiative, which we shall assume in accordance with divine judgement.[6]

In 410 Emperor Honorius passed a decree that said:

> Let all who act contrary to the scared laws know that their creeping in their heretical superstition to worship at the most remote oracle is punishable by exile and blood.[7]

By 435 a law was promulgated that threatened any heretic that was discovered in the empire, with death. The English word heresy comes from the Greek word *hairesis* which means 'choice'. So this legislation meant that, from then on, when it came to the matter of religion, the people in the empire had no choice.[8]

Pelagius, an Irish monk of 'high character', turned up in the city of Rome at the beginning of the fifth century, and took exception to the establishment over this issue of choice. He asserted that the concept of choice was essential to any meaningful notion of virtue or liberty. And he argued that if there was no place for choice, there was no place for virtue or liberty either. According to Pelagius, 'to be able to do good is the vestibule of virtue, and to be able to do evil is the evidence of liberty.'[9]

Augustine, the Bishop of Hippo, promptly denounced the ideas of the noble Pelagius as a danger to law and order. He declared that free will could very well undermine the foundation on which the empire was built. He contended that the use of force was necessary to compel all those people, involved in 'heresies and schisms', outside the fold of the true faith, to come in. And he concluded, adding insult to injury, by saying, 'let them [that are compelled] not find fault with being compelled!'[10] Those like Pelagius, who persisted in finding fault with 'being compelled', were excommunicated at Augustine's behest.[11]

From then on all public debate on religious subjects was banned.[12] Over 270,000 ancient documents, collected by Ptolemy Philadelphus, and 700,000 classical scrolls, kept in the Library of Alexandria, that were considered questionable, were burned.[13]

Emperors, popes, and power: ca. AD 500 – 1000

During this period, when the Roman Empire collapsed, and the Holy Roman Empire was created, Christianity continued to increase its power, as the church slowly but surely took control of the state. The western Roman Empire fell to the Christian Visigoths.[14] The eastern Roman Empire was hit by a devastating bout of the bubonic plague, which killed up to 10,000 people a day, is thought to have taken 100 million lives, and, the church said, was 'a punishment from God', because the state had not submitted to their authority.[15]

Both in the western and the eastern empires, people fled in terror to the Roman Catholic Church for the protection they promised.[16] And thus church control of the state was assured.[17] The theory of the plenitude of power gave the Pope, as Vicar of Christ, power over all earthly authorities, including the Emperor.[18] In an era when people believed in the divine right of kings, the approval of the Pope was paramount, so he was able to appoint and depose kings at will.[19]

This was best demonstrated in the celebrated coronation of Charlemagne, whom the Pope crowned with great pageantry in 800, as the undisputed Emperor of the Holy Roman Empire. As Phillip Schaff reported:

> To depose princes, to absolve subjects from allegiance, to actively foment rebellion, ... to give away crowns ... and consecrate armies ... to extort by threat of the payment of tribute, to punish dissenters with perpetual imprisonment, or turn them over to the authorities knowing death would be the punishment: these were the high prerogatives actually exercised by the papacy.[20]

Where there is power, there is always profit to be made. And as a result of the prerogatives they exercised, the church prospered. The church made money by selling franchises on ecclesiastical offices, peddling indulgences for the forgiveness of sins, collecting revenues from compliant imperial rulers, and confiscating disputed property, by force if necessary.[21] Not surprisingly, during this period the church managed to amass an enormous amount of capital. At one stage, it owned and operated between one-quarter and one-third of the entire land mass of western Europe—tax-free![22]

To groups like the Paulicans, the blatant collaboration of church and state, and the obvious abuse of papal and imperial power for

14

profit, were an abomination. The Paulicans, also known as the Bogomils, 'Those Who Prayed to God', (from the old Slavonic *Bogu*, to God, and *moliti*, to pray), were renowned for their piety.[23] They were so appalled by the impropriety displayed by the church, in collusion with the state, that they publicly declared that the established church had completely forfeited any right it may have had to be considered the 'true' church.[24]

The leaders of the established church replied that they, and they alone, had what was called 'the power of the keys', that is, possession of the keys to the kingdom of heaven, entrusted to them through apostolic succession by St. Peter. If the Bogomils wanted to be saved, then they should submit to the authority of the established church.[25]

But the Bogomils responded by saying that the only key to the kingdom that counted, was 'the key of truth', and that any claim to apostolic authority that was not backed up with some apostolic honesty and integrity, was a joke, and a bad joke at that. And they wanted nothing to do with it. [26]

So the People Who Prayed To God, said that from then on, people of faith should organise and manage their own autonomous communities of faith, separate from, and independent of, the machinations of church and state and their minions.[27] Soon, peaceful protest communities were springing up all over the place, like mushrooms. The church and state authorities were incensed by this simple but straightforward challenge to their divine right to rule. They quickly marshalled the battalions at their command, and in a series of ruthless orchestrated campaigns, crushed the People Who Prayed To God. Between 842 and 867 about 100,000 Bogomils were systematically slaughtered—beheaded, burned or drowned.[28]

Looking back, Gregory Magistros, himself in charge of one such bloody campaign of slaughter, wrote, 'They were given over to the sword, without pity, sparing neither the elderly nor the children, and ... quite rightly!'[29]

Crusades, inquisitions, and control: ca. AD 1000 – 1500

During the Middle Ages the church continued to strengthen its control by developing its own ecclesiastical judicial system, and expanding the scope of canon law to take in, then take over, civil law itself.[30] The church claimed jurisdiction in all cases in which it was involved.[31] The church also claimed jurisdiction in all cases where sacraments or oaths were involved.[32] Consequently 'there was scarcely a limit to [the church's] intervention; for in medieval society well-nigh everything was connected with a sacrament or depended on an oath.'[33]

The church expected complete obedience to its commands. It would tolerate nothing less than total submission to its dictates. In 1095 Pope Urban II called for a Crusade, or 'Holy War', to be led by 'Christian Knights', who would take up arms and sally forth to fight against the 'enemies of Christ'.[34] 'Cursed be the man who holds back his sword from shedding blood!' was the blood-curdling cry of Pope Gregory VII ringing in the the ears of the dedicated 'Soldier of Christ'.[35]

Over the course of the next two centuries, the 'soldiers of Christ' threw themselves, body and soul, into the task of killing thousands, if not millions, of 'heretics' and 'heathens'.[36] In 1096 the People's Crusade sacked Belgrade, which next to Constantinople, was the greatest non-Catholic Orthodox city in the world.[37] In 1204, the Crusaders attacked Constantinople itself, raping, pillaging and plundering this great Christian city in the name of Christ.[38] In the meantime, they also managed to assault the Holy City of Jerusalem, and slaughter its Jewish and Muslim inhabitants.[39]

It was a massacre. Nicetas Choniates, a Byzantine historian, wrote at the time with evident distress, that 'even the Saracens are merciful ... compared to these men who bear the Cross of Christ on their shoulders.'[40] But Raymond of Aguilers enthusiastically eulogised the massacre as 'a just and marvellous judgment of God':

> Wonderful things were to be seen. Numbers of Saracens were beheaded ... Others were shot with arrows, or forced to jump from towers; others were tortured for several days, then burned with flames. In the streets were seen piles of heads and hands and feet. One rode about everywhere amid the corpses of men and horses. In the Temple of Solomon [sic], the horses waded in blood up to their knees, nay, up to their bridle. *It was a just and marvellous judgement of God, that this place should be filled with the blood of unbelievers.*[41] (Author's emphasis)

In 1231 Pope Gregory IX officially established the Inquisition as an independent tribunal, responsible only to the pope, to inquire into any cases where acquiescence to prescribed views was suspect.[42] The Inquisition was the 'tribunal from hell'. The Inquisitor was selected not for his equanimity in judging a case, but for his enthusiasm in prosecuting a case. However, he acted as both prosecutor and judge.[43] The Inquisitor and his assistants were permitted to carry arms, and he was granted the right to absolve his assistants from any acts of violence, committed in pursuing the prosecution of a case.[44] In the Inquisition the common law right, to be presumed innocent until proven guilty, was set aside by the canon law order, to be presumed guilty, until proven innocent.[45] Names of witnesses against the accused were kept secret.[46] Horrific torture was officially approved, and frequently used, to ruthlessly extract a confession of guilt from the badly beaten victim.[47]

The Inquisition used every conceivable means to inflict unbearable pain on its prey, from dislocating limbs to dismembering bodies.[48] Some victims were tied up in ropes, immersed in water and slowly drowned, while others were covered in lard, set over a fire and slowly roasted.[49] One torture involved throwing a victim into a pit full of snakes. Another particularly gruesome torture involved turning a large dish full of mice upside down on the victim's stomach. A fire was then lit on top of the dish, causing the mice to panic and burrow into the stomach.'[50]

One way or another, in the end, nearly everyone confessed. So those thought by the Inquisitor to be guilty, were so judged by the Inquisition. The sentences that ensued were merciless. In 1244 the Council of Narbonne ordered that 'in the sentencing of heretics, no husband should be spared because of his wife, nor wife because of her husband, nor parent because of helpless children, and no sentence mitigated because of sickness or old age.'[51] All sentences included a mandatory flagellation, or flogging.[52] A common sentence was perpetual imprisonment, on a diet of bread and water, often in chains, and occasionally in solitary confinement.[53]

Then there was the stake. According to papal statutes, all unrepentent heretics had to be burnt at the stake alive.[54] To his endless shame the hopelessly misnamed pope, Innocent III, publicly proclaimed: 'anyone, who attempted to construe a personal view ... which conflicted with church dogma, must be burned without pity!'[55]

Worldwide evangelisation, witch hunts and genocide: ca. AD 1500 - 2000

In the last five centuries Christianity has spread worldwide. The sixteenth and seventeenth centuries saw an enormous upsurge of renewed energy and enthusiasm for evangelisation through the period of the Reformation and the Counter-Reformation.[56] By the middle of the eighteenth century Christianity had spread to all five continents, and was more widespread than any other religion had ever been.[57] By the middle of the twentieth century Christianity was still spreading. It now not only had more territory, it also had more adherents, and was more influential in world affairs than any other religion.[58]

Unfortunately, that influence included continued church collaboration with the state, utter disregard for human rights, total destruction of tribal cultures, and a direct and indirect involvement in genocide.

The famous Reformer, Martin Luther, advocated personal salvation for all people; but at the same time he supported the princes, who were his patrons, in their brutal suppression of the peasants when they tried to stand up for themselves and fight for some basic human rights.[59] Another famous Protestant, John Calvin, insisted on his right to oppose Catholicism; but like the Catholics he opposed, he sought to impose his views by force in the city where he lived, even to the point of having his opponents burnt at the stake.[60]

The notorious English Puritan leader, Oliver Cromwell, razed the ancient Irish city of Drogheda to the ground, slaughtered its 'Papist' inhabitants, and rejoiced in the 'righteous judgement of God' he had been able to bring 'upon these barbarous wretches'.[61]

Meanwhile Christopher Columbus landed in America, that he mistakenly took for India, and set about trying 'to convert the heathen Indians to our Holy Faith.'[62] While Columbus went about converting the Indians, he set all males over the age of fourteen to work, panning the rivers for gold for him. The work quotas set were too high, and almost impossible to meet. But those who did not meet them were accused of laziness, or worse still, of theft, and had their hands cut off. When the 'Indians' threatened to revolt because of their treatment, Columbus used their threats as an excuse to enslave them.[63] So much for the matter of 'our Holy Faith'.

'Conquistadors' like Hernando Cortes and Francisco Pizarro decided to follow in the 'glorious' footsteps of Christopher Columbus. Cortes made his way to Tenochtitlan, the capital city of the Aztec Empire, in present-day Mexico, where at first he was greeted with great acclaim as their god, Quetzalcoatl. He used the opportunity to capture their Emperor, Montezuma, and keep him as a hostage, so as to control the Aztec Empire. When the people rebelled, Cortes killed Montezuma, destroyed Tenochtitlan, and annexed the Aztec Empire, and eventually the whole of Mexico.[64]

Once the people were subdued, Peter of Ghent, one of the early missionaries, wrote that they were very easily converted:

> I and a brother who was with me in this province of Mexico baptised upwards of 200,000 persons—so many in fact I cannot give an accurate estimate of the number. Often we baptised in a single day 14,000 people ...[65]

While Cortes made his way to Tenochtitlan, Pizarro made his way to Cuzco, the capital city of the Inca Empire, in Peru. Unlike Cortes, Pizarro wasn't greeted like a god. But with a small contingent of men, Pizarro, like Cortes, was still able to capture the Emperor Atahuallpa and keep him as a hostage so as to control the Inca Empire. In spite of paying a vast ransom, rumoured to have included at least one room full of gold and two rooms full of silver, Atahuallpa, like Montezuma, was killed, and all Inca opposition, like all Aztec opposition, was crushed.[66] Again mass conversions quickly followed military conquest.[67] Those 'Indians' who did not convert, were burnt at the stake.[68]

As the 'conversion of the Indians' was considered to be the chief interest in the enterprise, to most Christians the exploits of Cortes and Pizarro were considered to be an extraordinary success.[69] It was left to a few, like Bartolomé de las Casas, a contemporary of Cortes and Pizarro, to lament that 'everything we have done to the Indians thus far was tyrannical and wrong!'[70]

It is worth noting that when the missionaries finally got to India, the Indians did not fare much better than the Aztecs or the Incas. Some 3,800 Goans were killed in the evangelisation of Goa.[71] When it came to my own country, Australia, it was the same old story all over again. Invaders took possession of the land and disposessed the indigenous tribal population. Those who had the temerity to resist were exterminated, and thousands of Aboriginal people were killed in the process.

While some Christians, like John Gribble, did protest the injustice, most did not. In fact, most Christians were more likely to voice their support for the invasion, in which they had a vested interest, and like John Dunmore Lang, were prepared to go to extraordinary lengths to try to rationalise the injustice that was done in the name of God:

[We] have only carried out the intention of the Creator in coming and settling down in the territory of the natives. God's first command to man was 'Be fruitful - multiply and replenish the earth'. Now that the aborigine has not done, and therefore it was no fault in taking the land of which they were previously possessors.[72]

And so the Christian road show rolled on, crushing anyone that happened to get in the way.

While Christianity was extending its control, it was also tightening its control around the world by conducting witch-hunts whereever it went. Pope John XXII had officially sanctioned witch-hunts when he authorised the persecution of witchcraft.[73] Witchcraft was held to be the cause behind all sorts of calamities. The obvious solution to a problem was to find the witch responsible.

Once accused of witchcraft it was virtually impossible to escape conviction. Ordinary warts, freckles, and birthmarks were all considered proof of extraordinary perversity.[74] A physician working in prisons where women accused of witchcraft were kept, said they were driven mad 'by frequent torture ... kept in prolonged squalor and darkness of their dungeons ... and constantly dragged out to undergo atrocious torment.'[75] A dissident priest said at the time that the 'wretched creatures are compelled by the severity of the torture to confess to things they have never done, and so, by cruel butchery, innocent lives are taken.'[76]

From the terrible Basque witch-hunt in Old World Catalonia, to the sensational Salem witch-hunts in New World Massachusetts, countless innocent people were killed in witch-hunts around the world.[77] The scripture text most quoted by most eager witch-hunters was: 'Rebellion is as the sin of witchcraft!' (1 Samuel 15:23)[78]

So, lest they be accused of 'rebellion', the 'sin of witchcraft', people made sure that they did their very best to be compliant, and to avoid any appearance of disputation with the authorities. Thus witch-hunts proved to be, as one contemporary witness wryly observed, a very potent mechanism of effective political control:

Preachers do not dare preach, and those who preach do not dare to touch on contentious matters, for their lives are in the mouths of ignoramuses, and nobody is without a policeman.[79]

Rossell Hope Robbins called this 'shocking nightmare' of total suppression, caused by the witch hunts that were prosecuted from the fifteenth right through to the eighteenth century, 'the foulest crime and deepest shame of western civilisation.'[80] But the worst was yet to come: the Holocaust.

In the middle of the twentieth century, six million Jewish men, women and children were systematically tagged with yellow stars, then dragged out, beaten up, and shot, or rounded up like animals, thrown onto cattle trucks, and herded into concentration camps, where the 'productive' were put to work in slave battalions, and the 'unproductive' put to death in gas chambers.

It was the worst single atrocity that our world has ever known. The Holocaust, as it came to be called, was characterised by an extraordinary degree of savagery. According to Albert Fischer, one of the German staff at the Main Supply Camp for Treblinka:

> Brutality was the air Jews breathed, ... beating was the camp's invariable daily fare ... One particularly brutal sergeant, Max Dietrich, [was] a paragon of the camp's brutality. Dietrich, with a leather whip, flogged Jews fearfully. [One day] I saw Dietrich beat [a] Jew so long until he lay unconscious on the ground. Then Dietrich ordered other Jews to fully undress the unconscious Jew and to pour water over him. When the Jew regained consciousness, Dietrich grabbed the hands of the Jew, who had defecated all over himself, dunked them in the excrement and forced him to eat the excrement ... [By] that evening ... this Jewish worker, nourished on his own excrement, was dead.[81]

The Holocaust was characterised not only by an extraordinary degree of savagery, but also by an extraordinarily casual attitude towards endemic cruelty. Take for example the case of Julius and Vera Wohlauf, and how this young German couple decided to spend their honeymoon:

Captain Wohlauf, the commander of First Company, [Police Battalion 101,] had [his] wife by [his] side while they were killing [Jews] in Poland. Wohlauf had earlier returned to Hamburg, shortly after Police Battalion 101 arrived in Poland, in order to go through with an already scheduled wedding. ... He then caught up with his comrades ... She [also] stayed with the battalion for at least several weeks and several killing operations, and [actually] participated in one, maybe two, of the large ones.

Wohlauf's wife attended the day-long killing operation that the entire battalion conducted at Miedzyrzec on August 25 [1942]. The roundup, the driving of the Jews from their homes into the market square, was perhaps the most brutal that Police Battalion 101 conducted. The men left hundreds of dead Jews strewn about the streets. The scene at the market square was also amongst the most gruesome. Some of the notable features included the Germans forcing Jews to squat for hours in the burning sun so that many fainted, and shooting any Jew who did nothing more than stand up. The market square became littered with the dead. Such shootings naturally included many children who found it particularly difficult to remain immobile in such discomfort for hours on end.

Frau Wohlauf was a party to all this, [and], if conforming to her usual practice, probably carried that symbol of domination, a riding whip, with her ... [while] Miedzyrzec's German Gendarmerie ... entertained themselves by flogging Jews with [their] whips. That day she ... and the wives of some other locally stationed Germans, as well as a group of German Red Cross nurses ... got to observe first-hand how their men were purging the world of the putative Jewish menace, by killing around one thousand and deporting ten thousand more to their deaths. This is how the pregnant Frau Wohlauf spent her honeymoon.[82]

Daniel Jonah Goldhagen, in his recent, much lauded, but most disturbing book on the Holocaust, aptly entitled *Hitler's Willing Executioners*, writes:

Jewish survivors report with virtual unanimity German cruelties right until the very end. They leave no doubt that the Germans were seething in hatred for their victims. The Germans were not emotionally neutral executors of superior orders, or cognitively neutral bureaucrats indifferent to the nature of their deeds. The Germans chose to act as they did with no effectual supervision, guided only by their comprehension of the world, by their own notions of justice.[83]

The question of course is – why? Why did the Germans hate the Jews so much? Why did something as obviously wrong as slaughtering six million Jews seem the right thing for them to do at the time? This the question Goldhagen seeks to answer. His conclusion is simply this: 'that "ordinary Germans" were animated by antisemitism', by 'a particular type of antisemitism', what he refers to as 'eliminationist antisemitism', that led them to conclude 'that the Jews *ought to die*.'[84]

Goldhagen then cites not Hitler, not the Nazis, not the S.S. stormtroopers, but Christianity, as 'the single most powerful cause for producing endemic antisemitism in the Christian world.'[85]

To start with, he says, Christians saw Jews as 'Christ-killers' and 'Christians conceived of their religion as superseding Judaism. Therefore Jews, as Jews, ought to disappear from the earth.'[86] Then Martin Luther, the 'great reformer', who laid the spiritual foundations of the modern German state, turned out to be the 'greatest antisemite of his time.'[87] 'Never once', he says, 'did any German Bishop, Catholic or Protestant speak on publicly on behalf of the Jews, as did the French Archbishop of Toulouse.'[88] Instead both Bishop Dibelius and Bishop Sasse publicly expressed a hope of a 'solution' to the 'Jewish problem', that augmented the Nazi propaganda programme, saying, that they simply 'wished them (that is, the Jews) to die out.'[89]

Thus, Goldberg says, 'the church became a compliant helper of Nazi Jewish policy'.[90]

Looking back on the Holocaust in a lecture he gave in March 1946, Pastor Martin Niemuller foreshadowed Goldhagen's findings when he confessed that 'Christianity in Germany bears a greater responsibility before God than the Nazis, the S.S. and the Gestapo. Are not we Christians much more to blame, am I not much more guilty,' he asks, 'than many who bathed their hands in blood?'[91]

One would have hoped that Christians had learnt something from the salutory lesson of being implicated as 'the single most powerful cause' of 'the worst single atrocity that the world has ever known'. But I am not so sure that we have learnt anything at all. At the end of the twentieth century Christians are still actively supporting genocidal policies in the name of Christ. We all know about the part the church has performed in supporting apartheid in South Africa, and the bloodshed in Northern Ireland. But how many of us know about the role that U.S. evangelicals have played in Central America, supporting brutal government and guerrilla groups, regularly cited by Amnesty International for serious ongoing abuses of human rights?

In El Savador, U.S. evangelicals worked directly with the Salvadorean military, 'shoulder to shoulder with the same men who slit throats in the darkness of the night.'[92] At one stage the Salvadorean military even made a helicopter available for the Christian Anti-Communist Crusade (sic) to drop anti-communist propaganda over villages held by the FMLN (the Farabundo Marti National Liberation Front).[93] On one mission Paralife Ministries evangelist, John Steer, toured some eight miltary bases and spoke to over three and a half thousand military personnel, telling them: 'killing for the joy of it was wrong, but killing because it was necessary to fight against an anti-Christ system, communism, was not only right, but the duty of every Christian.'[94]

In Nicaragua, U.S evangelicals, like Colonel Oliver North, worked directly for the CIA with the anti-communist contras, transferring millions of dollars of profits from the sale of U.S.arms to Iran, to support the contras in their fight against the Sandanistas.[95] At the same time, Pat Robertson, on the '700 Club', a U.S. show produced by CBN, (the Christian Broadcasting Network), made an appeal for more U.S. aid to the contras.[96] CBN contributed three million dollars itself to the Nicaraguan Patriotic Association, an organisation connected to the contras.[97]

In Guatemala, U.S. evangelicals worked directly with the Guatemalan military. During this period, with the support of U.S. evangelicals, the Guatemalan military killed between three and ten thousand civilians.[98] In 1976 an American group called Gospel Outreach travelled to Guatemala to do relief work. While they were there they converted a man by the name of Efrain Rios Montt to their cause.[99]

27

In 1982, as a result of a military coup, Rios Montt, an army general, was asked to take power. After consulting with his advisors at Gospel Outreach, Rios Montt accepted the proposal, and so became the first 'born-again' President of Guatemala.[100] U.S. evangelicals were ecstatic. In June 1982 Rios Montt's aide met with US evangelical leaders, including Loren Cunningham, the Director of Youth With A Mission, to rally support for the regime.[101] At one point, a battalion of missionary volunteers, and aid of a billion dollars, were promised to support 'God's miracle in Guatemala'.[102]

The first act of the 'born-again' President of Guatemala, was to suspend the constitution.[103] His next act was to unleash a campaign of genocidal terror against the native population of Guatemala.[104] According to *Garrison Guatemala*, 'entire Indian villages were erased from the map.'[105] The *Americas Watch* human rights report records: 'the army does not waste its bullets on women and children. We were repeatedly told of women being raped before being killed, and of children being picked up by the feet and having their heads smashed against walls ...'[106] A Pastor of Gospel Outreach's Verbo Church explained the actions of their charge, by saying, 'We hold Brother Efrain Rios Montt like King David in the Old Testament. He is the King of the New Testament. The army doesn't massacre the Indians. It massacres demons, and the Indians are demon-possessed. They are communists.'[107]

In recent days there has been no greater tragedy in Christianity than the genocide in Rwanda. I can remember growing up on stories of the 'Great East African Revival', an evangelical renewal movement that swept through Rwanda a generation ago, that Christian pundits at the time predicted would 'bring the light of Christ to the dark continent of Africa.' I don't know what effect the 'Great East African Revival' had, but I do know that barely a generation later, after the evangelical renewal had come and gone, in early April 1994, the country of Rwanda was engulfed in a frenzy of tribal violence, that erupted into the worst case of tribal warfare in Africa's history.[108] Over half of the entire population of Rwanda were forced to flee for their lives, and one million people—men, women, and children who could neither run nor hide—were pitilessly put to death.[109]

While many Christians, particularly the Quakers and the Seventh-Day Adventists, acted heroically trying to save people who were being attacked—and were themselves hacked to death, along with the neighbours they sought to protect—both Catholics and Protestants had 'key leaders' who not only 'did not speak out against the killings' but actually 'promoted the genocide' for their own purposes.[110] Reverend Tokenboh Adeyemo, the Director of the Association of Evangelicals in Africa, says that 'homogeneous church growth' resulted in the growth of ethnic churches. This only served to fan the flame of tribal rivalry, and contribute to the final tribal conflagration.[111]

In fact the most recent research by Dr John Steward seems to indicate—much to the shame of the Christian community—that it was 'the Muslims who came out of the genocide "cleaner" than the Christians!'[112] Unlike the Christians, Muslims 'are said to have not participated in the killings!'[113]

This brief reflection on the history of the cuelty that runs like a thick blood-red thread through the tapestry of the history of Christianity, does not discount the countless acts of charity done by caring Christians through the ages. But it does confront us, as it once did Thomas Jefferson, with the truth that:

Millions of innocent men, women, and children, since the introduction of Christianity, have been burnt, tortured, fined,

and imprisoned ... [And] what has been the effect of [this]
coercion?To make half the world fools and the other half
hypocrites [and] to support error and roguery all over the
earth.[114]

Christianity on Trial: Guilty as Charged?

Christianity is still probably the dominant religion in the world. So it is absolutely vital for the future welfare of the human family, that we examine the serious charges of continued church collaboration with the state, utter disregard for human rights, total destruction of tribal cultures, and direct and indirect involvement in genocide, that we have put forward against it.

The charges themselves are obviously undeniable. And in my experience, Christians don't tend to *deny* them. However, they do tend to *discount* them: either by generally emphasizing the positive influence rather than the negative effect of Christianity, or by explaining that for each atrocity committed by a Christian, there was a particular set of extenuating circumstances that make the act understandable, if not excusable.

For example, if you say something about the Crusades or the Inquisition, most Christians will say things like: 'it was a long time ago', 'times were different then', 'people didn't know any better', 'the people who committed those crimes against humanity must have been crazy', 'they weren't really Christians, you know,' 'if you want to know what real Christianity is all about, forget the Crusades and the Inquisition and consider the example of Mother Teresa and the Missionaries of Charity.'

None of these comments actually denies the fact that atrocities were committed in the name of Christianity. But they all attempt to discount the significance of these atrocities as true indicators of the nature of Christianity. Now this brings us face to face with the life-and-death question, at the very heart of the matter, that we desperately need to answer: *Are the atrocities done in the name of Christianity, true indicators of the nature of Christianity, or not?* If the answer to this question is that these atrocities are *not* true indicators, but mere aberrations, then we have nothing to fear from the continued expansion of Christianity.

But if the answer to this question is, as I suspect, that these cruelties *are* true indicators—inevitable, albeit unintended, consequences of the religion as it really is—then we have everything to fear from the triumph of Christianity in the coming millennium. To answer this question we will need to consider a range of personal, political, and spiritual perspectives, then assess how significant Christianity itself is, as an explanation of the cause of these events.

Some personal perspectives: evil, fear, avarice, power, and the authoritarian personality

All the personal interpretations of the atrocities done in the name of Christ, would suggest that the real explanation for any action has more to do with people's personalities than their religion.

The controversial American psychiatrist, Scott Peck, suggests that there are some people who are actually 'evil'. People who are 'evil', Peck says, are people 'who refuse to face their own sin, project blame onto others, and scapegoat others to such an extent that they will use whatever power they have at their disposal to destroy the objects of their blame'.[1] Hitler immediately comes to mind. So also does the particularly brutal anti-semitic German sergeant, Max

Dietrich, who killed his Jewish prisoner by forcing him to eat his own excrement.

However, not all those involved in the atrocities we are contemplating, even the Wohlaufs, could be considered 'evil' in this classic pathological sense. Some were caught up in the perpetration of these atrocities out of fear: either fear of their enemies, or fear of themselves, or both. You could argue that Augustine had Pelagius excommunicated because he was not only afraid of Pelagius, but also afraid of the implications of Pelagian doctrine for himself. Apparently Augustine, in stark contrast to the noble Pelagius, had led a very promiscuous life in his youth, siring, and then abandoning, an illegitimate child. Augustine had found it impossible for him to control his sexual impulses, no matter how hard he had tried. And he had come to the conclusion that sexual impulses were uncontrollable. 'Who can control this when its appetite is aroused?' he asked. 'No one!' he exclaimed. 'No one!' 'In the very movement of this appetite, then, it has no mode that that responds to the decision of the will ...'[2] So you can imagine how Augustine must have felt when someone like Pelagius turned up, who not only preached free will, but also practised it to a degree that he had thought was impossible. Augustine was scared of Pelagius: scared that his piety would unmask his own impiety, scared that his discipline would expose his own unwillingness to deal with his own sexuality responsibly. So Augustine had Pelagius excommunicated.

Some, like the Inquisitors, got caught up in the cycle of violence, not through fear, but through their own avarice. Inquisitors grew very rich very quickly. 'They received bribes from the wealthy who escaped accusation.' And they confiscated the the property of the accused. As there was little chance of the accused being proven innnocent, there was no need to wait for conviction to confiscate the property.[3] Inquisitors rarely shared their ill-gotten gains with the episcopal or the imperial courts, as was originally expected. They 'seize[d] everything for [them]selves, not even sending a share to the officials of the Inquisition at Rome'.[4]

Some, like the Conquistadors, got caught up in the cycle of violence, not only through their avarice, but also through their unbridled lust for power. Columbus proudly crowed of how he 'took [his] pleasure' with a native woman in his power, after 'soundly' whipping her with a piece of rope.[5] And Cortes could arrogantly brag about becoming 'the most powerful man in the New World', owning more than twenty thousand slaves whose sole purpose in life was simply to do his bidding. [6]

The acclaimed British psychiatrist, Jack Dominion, suggests that some people seem to have 'authoritarian personalities'. An authoritarian personality tends to be

> more secure when he has his niche within a hierarchy, is submissive and respectful to those above him, and contemptuous and dictatorial to those below him, repressive of his own instincts, is generally in favour of discipline, and is punitive towards 'sinners', particularly if they are judged to be 'inferior' in any way.[7]

According to Dominion, 'it does not require much imagination to see that Christianity, as [it is] popularly conceived by its most zealous adherents, would include in its ranks such authoritarian personalities' as Martin Luther, John Calvin, and Oliver Cromwell, who would 'use Christ as symbol to support just about everything that would have been repudiated as a proper Christian attitude by the originator of that faith'[8].

Some political perspectives: evil, hysteria, charisma, sanctions, and the totalitarian political economy

All the political interpretations of the atrocities done in the name of Christ would suggest that the real explanation for any action has more to do with people's politics than their religion.

I would suggest that people can be evil, not only personally, but also politically. In fact I would argue that such evil may be defined as 'the exercise of political power that imposes one's will upon others, by overt or covert coercion, without due regard for love and justice'.[9] The Crusades immediately come to mind. When a cluster of small Italian towns sought to throw off the yoke of the tyranny of the Catholic Church in 1375, the pope's legate in Italy, Robert of Geneva, hired an army of mercenaries, and set about taking revenge on the little town of Cesena.

> Swearing clemency by a solemn oath on his cardinal's hat, Cardinal Robert persuaded the men of Cesena to lay down their arms, and won their confidence by asking for fifty hostages and immediately releasing them as evidence of good will. Then summoning his mercenaries ... he ordered a general massacre 'to exercise justice'.
>
> For three days and nights beginning February 3, 1377, while the city gates were closed, the soldiers slaughtered. 'All the squares were full of dead.' Trying to escape, hundreds drowned in the moats, thrust back by relentless swords. Women were seized for rape, ransom was placed on children, plunder succeeded the killing, 'and what could not be carried away, they burned, made unfit for use, or spilled upon the ground.' The toll of the dead was between 2,500 and 5,000.[10]

For me this episode is the epitome of personal and political evil.

However, not all those involved in the atrocities we are contemplating could be considered 'evil'; some were caught up in the perpetration of these atrocities through hysteria. Elias Canetti, in his book *Crowds and Power*, analyses the way in which ordinary people can be caught up in a crowd, and through crowd hysteria— which simultaneously increases their sense of power, and decreases their sense of responsibility—can commit extraordinary crimes against humanity.[11]

In England, where there was no official programme for prosecuting witches, many women were still killed as witches, by mobs. A common practice was to 'swim a witch': a mob would take a woman, accused of witchcraft, bind her hand and feet, and throw her into some water to see if she could 'swim'. If the woman was rejected by the water, the medium of holy baptism, and floated to the top, she would be pronounced guilty, and would be promptly killed by the mob. However, if the woman was embraced by the holy waters of baptism, and sank to the bottom, she would be pronounced innocent, and would be posthumously acclaimed by the mob.[12] Either way the hysterical crowd got their corpse.

Some people became involved in committing some of the atrocities we are considering because they were dazzled by the charisma of a dynamic leader who insisted that they take part. Max Weber, in his *Theory Of Social And Economic Organisations*, says that leaders with charisma have an 'aura of magic about them', and that people can be so strongly attracted to this charisma or powerful personal magnetism, that, to their devotees, such leaders may prove to be irresistible.[13] Loren Cunningham is one such charismatic leader. He has the capacity to take complete command of an audience, and totally convince them that his agenda is theirs. Pat Robertson is another such charismatic leader, who has augmented his powerful personal magnetism with even more powerful propaganda techniques, such as framing a 'debate' with two nearly identical 'sides', and demonising anyone who would beg to disagree, so he seldom loses an argument.[14] As for Efrain Rios Montt, just ask his pastor. 'He is a King, a new King David, who will defeat the Enemy, and lead the Chosen Ones to victory!' So if he says it's necessary to massacre the Indians (in order to 'massacre the demons', because 'the Indians are demon-possessed'), then it must be necessary to massacre the Indians.[15]

Some people became involved in committing some of the atrocities we are considering because they were driven by the sanctions they were threatened with if they did not get involved. Gene Sharp, in his book *Power and Struggle*, analyses the way that subjects can be compelled by rulers, who have power over them, to act in compliance with a directive, even when it contravenes every standard of common human decency. After all, 'sanctions', he says, 'are an enforcement of obedience.'[16]

Excommunication is a sanction that the church has used to great effect through the centuries. I know from my own experience just how difficult it is refuse to obey a direct order when the consequences of disobedience may be the loss of all that is dear to you. Execution has always been the ultimate sanction that the church and the state have used to enforce total obedience. As the Inquisitor Francisco Pena proclaimed, 'We must remember that the main purpose of the trial and execution is not to save the soul of the accused but to ... put fear into others.'[17] Only those of us who have been threatened with execution, will know how effective the fear of execution is in enforcing obedience.

The American theologian, Walter Wink, says that most people are part of totalitarian political economies that determine the way they live their lives. 'No social system, to be sure, has ever been purely totalitarian. Even in the most oppressively patriarchal structures, women and men continue to dream of a more equitable way ... But, once states arose,' Wink says, 'new myths were created to socialise [subjects] into their inferior status. [And] priesthoods, backed up by armies, courts and executioners, inculcated in people's minds terrible fear'. 'Thus', he says, 'people have become slaves of their evolving systems.' These systems, he says, are 'not hostile to human welfare; simply indifferent':[18] indifferent to pain, suffering, and to sorrow. Hence even fine Christians who are part of these systems have tended to be indifferent to cries for mercy from the countless innocent men, women, and children who have been killed through the centuries 'for the good of the cause'.

Some spiritual perspectives: the devil, illusion, desire, ethos and orthodox Christian theology

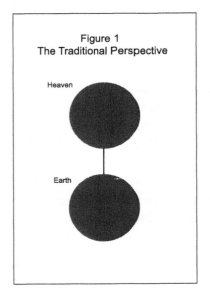

Figure 1
The Traditional Perspective

Heaven

Earth

There are four different spiritual perspectives, which seek to explain the relationship between the world of the spirit and the world of matter, and in particular the atrocities committed in the name of Christ, that we are considering.

The first spiritual perspective is the Traditional Perspective[19] (see Figure 1). This perspective sees reality in terms of two parallel dimensions, a heavenly one and an earthly one, which intersect and interact, and simultaneously reflect and reinforce the actions of one in the other. From the Traditional Perspective, the atrocities we are contemplating, could be seen as earthly skirmishes in a heavenly war between God and the Devil, as Frank Peretti sees them in his best selling contemporary novels, *This Present Darkness* and *Piercing The Darkness*.[20] Certainly people like Martin Luther and John Calvin saw their battles precisely in

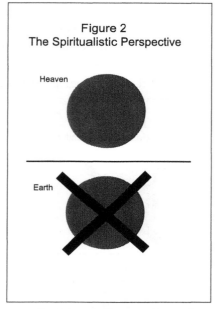

Figure 2
The Spiritualistic Perspective

Heaven

Earth

these terms. Luther said that 'we are all subject to the Devil.'[21] Calvin said that the task of every saint is to engage in 'unceasing struggle against the Devil.'[22]

The second spiritual perspective is the Spiritualistic Perspective[23] (see Figure 2). This perspective also sees reality in terms of two parallel dimensions, a heavenly one that is manifest in the soul, and an earthly one that is manifest in the body. The heavenly dimension is 'real' and 'right', while the earthly dimension is 'unreal' and/or 'wrong'.

From the Spiritualistic Perspective, the atrocities we are contemplating could be seen, as they are by Baba Ram Das, in his cult classic, *Be Here Now*, as nothing but a bad dream, from which we will eventually awake to the realisation that 'pleasure and pain, loss and gain, fame and shame, are all the same—they're just happening.'[24] Certainly people like the Gnostic Monoimus and Meister Eckhart saw matters precisely in these terms. They believed that 'enlightenment' would dispel the 'ignorance' that produced a 'nightmarish existence' and 'experiences of terror'. [25]

The third spiritual perspective, the Materialistic Perspective, is the exact opposite of the Spiritualistic Perspective[26] (see Figure 3). The earthly dimension is 'real' and 'right', while the heavenly dimension is 'unreal' and/or 'wrong'. From the Materialistic Perspective, the atrocities we are contemplating, could be seen as nothing but 'fulfilments of the oldest, strongest and most urgent wishes of mankind', as seen by Sigmund Freud in his famous text on *The Future Of Illusion*.[27] Certainly people like Karl Marx and Friederich Engels saw the issues precisely in these terms. They said that the so called 'religious' character of many of these activities was 'simply a sacred cloak to hide desires that are very secular.'[28]

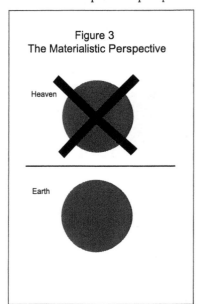

Figure 3
The Materialistic Perspective

Heaven

Earth

The fourth type of spiritual perspective is the Integral Perspective.[29] (see Figure 4). This perspective sees reality in terms of two coterminous aspects of the universe: an outer or earthly one, and an inner or heavenly one, so that every event has both an outer visible 'material' aspect and an inner invisible 'spiritual' aspect. From the Integral Perspective, the atrocities we are contemplating could be seen as destructive material expressions of demonic spiritual realities, 'that are actually parts of a single realm, [though] at present, they may appear to separate' as written by Morton Kelsey, in his beautiful book, *The Other Side Of Silence*.[30] People like Walter Wink and Charles Elliott see the events precisely in these terms. Walter Wink says, 'institutions have an actual spiritual ethos and we neglect this aspect of institutional life to our peril'.[31] Charles Elliott says, 'we have to return to the basic position that demonic powers control [church and state] structures, and it is those powers that have to be confronted if the structures are to be set free' from their destructive proclivities.[32]

Some Christians see the atrocities done in the name of Christ as having 'nothing to do with Christianity' because the atrocities

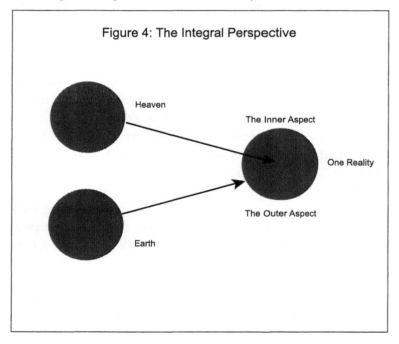

Figure 4: The Integral Perspective

are 'un-Christlike', and so by definition 'un-Christian'. Kenneth Latourette, the respected author of the comprehensive two-volume *A History Of Christianity*, often remarked after describing a disgraceful episode in the history of Christianity, that it was actually done by people who, 'although nominally Christian, denied it by their conduct.'[33] I have great sympathy for this view myself. But it assumes that a Christian is by definition Christlike, and anyone who would act in a manner that is not Christlike is by definition not a Christian. Now if this were true, I would have no worries about Christianity.

But it is not true. And very few Christians would say it was true. Because, they would explain, 'Christlikeness is not the reality which Christians personify, but the ideal to which Christians aspire'. So the vast majority of Christians, sooner or later, would sadly concede that it is not only possible, but it is also probable, that Christians, who are not yet Christlike, could commit the atrocities that we are considering. The question of course is why? Why would Christians, not just nominal Christians, but real Christians who ostensibly aspire to be like Christ, continue to commit such grievous crimes against humanity, as regularly as they do?

I think that the explanations that we have explored so far do answer that question to a certain extent. It is clear that 'real Christians', who aspire to be like Christ, all too easily often capitulate to terrible personal and political evil. Many are part of totalitarian political economies. Some develop authoritarian personalities themselves. Others are seduced by an intoxicating cocktail of fear and avarice and power. And still others are coerced by an overwhelming combination of hysteria and charisma and sanctions.

But you may well ask: why doesn't Christianity, which is meant to vouchsafe virtue, save Christians, who are supposed to be 'living

in the light', from succumbing en masse to the 'forces of darkness'?
One answer is, as we have seen, that *it is all an illusion*. A narrative,
'full of sound and fury, signifying nothing.' Now this answer is
really a non-answer, and in any case, it isn't true.

Another answer is that *Christianity is just an excuse that Christians
use to justify otherwise unjustifiable actions*. The Official List of Christian
Excuses includes two all-time favourites: 'The Lord told me to do
it!' and/or 'The Devil made me do it!' Now this answer – at least
the second bit of it – may be at best half the truth; but it is certainly
not anywhere near the whole truth.

Last, but not least, is the answer to the question that Christians
want to avoid at all costs: *that Christianity as a religion is not merely an
excuse, but actually the reason that so many Christians act in an un-Christlike
manner.* At a quick glance, any such suggestion might be considered by
most Christians to be heresy, even blasphemy. But, as I take the stand,
I put my hand on the Bible, I cross my heart, and I swear that it is the
truth, the whole truth, and nothing but the truth. So help me God.

Christians have consistently been shown to be un-Christlike.
Christians have constantly been shown to be dogmatic,[34]
judgmental,[35] and consequently quite intolerant of political dissent.[36]
Christians have constantly been shown to be more egocentric,[37] more
ethnocentric,[38] and, consequently, more uncharitable towards
disreputable minorities than their non-Christian compatriots.[39] 'The
more popular Christianity as a religion has become, the less likely
Christians have been to champion important unpopular campaigns,
like a due regard for universal basic human rights.'[40] Once Christianity
has become established as a religion, Christians have usually been
totally unwilling to advocate crucial anti-establishment causes, like
liberty, equality, and democracy for all.[41]

Sometimes, Christianity has served as 'the opiate of the people'.
At other times, it has acted as 'a benzedrine for brutality', which

has unleashed such a rush of unconscionable cruelty on such a massive scale that Christians have shamelessly slaughtered entire civilisations in frenzies of righteous indignation.[42]
To the victims, Christianity is the Antichrist!

Three witnesses: Morris West, Dudley Hyde, and Peter Cameron

Consider the testimony of three witnesses. All three of these witnesses are contemporary committed Christians. West is a Catholic, Hyde a Methodist, and Cameron a Presbyterian.

All of them have had ongoing conflicts with Christianity as a religion. But none of them has given up their faith in Christ. All of them, from time to time, have been accused of 'heresy'. But none of them have taken the charge lying down. West wrote his drama, *The Heretic*, in defence of dissent. Hyde, in his old age, penned a book that he subtitled *A Heretic's Handbook*, as a primer on protest for the younger generation. And Cameron, the only person I know of in my country to be officially charged and convicted of heresy this century, wrote an autobiography, aptly entitled the *Heretic*, in which he argues that it is so-called orthodox Christianity which is 'the most virulent heresy of all'.

Morris West is one of Australia's best-loved and best-selling writers. He has written over thirty books, many of which have been made into movies. His twenty-six novels have been translated into twenty-five languages, and sold over sixty million copies. Among his most distinguished works are his internationally-renowned inspirational religious quartet: *The Devil's Advocate, The Shoes Of The Fisherman, The Clowns Of God,* and *Lazarus.*

West was born in 1916 into an Irish Australian Catholic family. He says 'we were an excluded and exclusive community'.[43] When

44

he was not yet fourteen, West joined the Congregation of the Christian Brothers of Ireland. 'I see it now as a seduction of the young and immature into a choice they were quite unready to make.'[44] 'My earliest education grounded me in prejudice, which means pre-judgment, unexamined conviction. My later training as a novice was—let me say it baldly—an excercise in bigotry. All non-Christians were infidels.' [45] 'When Catholics were persecuted they were martyrs. When Simon de Montfort slaughtered the Albgensians he was a godly knight.'[46]

West stayed with the Christian Brothers for the next twelve years. until, on the eve of his final vows, he decided not to continue with the Congregation:

In the Congregation, I had my first experience of techniques designed to wash the human brain and bend the human spirit. They were practised by the novice master, who [was] an ignorant man, anti-intellectual, who did grave and sometimes irreparable damage to many of the youths in his charge. He humiliated them with gross penances: shaving their heads, sentencing them to extra field labour, making them take meal after meal on their knees. He tyrannised them with spiritual fears: damnation in every sexual thought, double damnation for every impulse of revolt. He was the first official intimidator I met. I have hated the breed ever since, be they bureaucrats or bullying army sergeants. I knew I could never believe in the God he preached. To reach the calm in which, thank God, I now reside, I have learned to forgive him. What I cannot forgive, and what I can never condone, is the impersonal cruelty which many institutions—my own church among them—practise upon their members, and which they justify by a thousand arguments, none of which I find acceptable. I have fought this cruelty all my life.[47]

Dudley Hyde is a Methodist minister who was director of youth work and Christian education in schools in New South Wales, and later, director in charge of Christian education in schools on behalf of all the Protestant Churches in Victoria, Australia.

Hyde was born in 1908. Neither of his parents were particularly religious. 'I don't remember my parents ever in church. My father, well, the first time he set foot in a church was when my mother died.'[48] There were ten children in the family. 'Only a couple of us got bitten by the religious bug in a big way. But I got the bug badly. It was not a half-hearted affair. I was proud of my fundamentalism.'[49]

Hyde went to Leigh Theological College. 'I knew, in fact, it was a hotbed of heresy, and I was determined to uproot these insidious heretics.'[50] But by May 1931, barely fifteen months after beginning his college course, Hyde found he could no longer continue as a fundamentalist, and he wrote to the faculty saying that now, as a thoroughly modern modernist, he could not 'accept the dogma of the church.' He says,

> It was virtually a suicide note. I was suspended from college indefinitely. I guess I saw myself as a martyr. I was on the 'wrong track' theologically, but the 'remedy' was to expel me from the very place where I might learn better. The Methodist Church expelled me. The problem was I still wanted to be a Methodist minister, but the church showed little sign of wanting me.

'How', he wondered 'to get back to college and yet keep some vestige of dignity?' At that time, he says, 'expediency began to take over from honesty.'

I went for counsel to an ex-President of the Methodist Church of Australia, in fact, an ex-President-General (of the Methodist Church). You can't go much higher than that, short of going all the way to God. I found him a very busy person, rather exasperated at my intrusion in his study. He had a quick, simple prescription for me: 'Draft another statement of your beliefs and send it to the committee that sacked you. Don't use any negatives. Mention only positives. If you can, include some Bible references, or even a quote from one of John Wesley's sermons.'

Hyde followed this advice, and the committee, upon reading his statement, promptly decided to reverse its decision, and reinstate him. Looking back, Hyde recalls the moment as 'a moment of triumph.' But

the price I paid was that I never thought the same about the church again, nor about my commitment to it. I had little respect for it. Disillusionment had taken over. Honesty had become a faded dream. [And] ministry had become a tawdry joke. In the institution we call the 'church' there are lots of rewards. People will sincerely welcome you. They love outsiders who genuinely want to be insiders. They may fawn on you and do all sorts of things to welcome you. And we all like being welcomed! But beware of the price of the 'free lunch'. The price is conformity. Growing [to be] like the people we are with. Soon you find yourself talking their language, singing their songs, even subscribing to their beliefs, because you don't want to be 'the odd one out'. I never overcame my sense of guilt at my hypocrisy.[51]

Peter Cameron studied law and theology at Edinburgh University, and practised both as a lawyer and a theologian before being appointed to the Meldrum Lectureship at Edinburgh University. In 1991 Cameron came to Australia to serve as the Principal of St. Andrew's College in the University of Sydney. In 1993 he was charged with, and convicted, of 'heresy' in a celebrated ecclesiastical trial that attracted huge media coverage, and caught the nation's attention.

In his defence, Cameron cites a disturbing story told by Dostoevsky. It is a story in Dostoevsky's *The Brothers Karamazov* about Christ coming back to earth during the time of the Spanish Inquisition, called 'the Legend of the Grand Inquisitor'.

Christ appears in Seville the day after a hundred heretics have been burned at the stake in a great *auto-da-fe*. He appears as he did during his lifetime, and the crowds recognise him at once, and he heals the sick. At the steps of the cathedral he meets the funeral procession for a little girl, and he has compassion on the mother and brings the child back to life. Just at that moment the Grand Inquisitor is passing and sees what has happened and orders his guards to arrest Christ and throw him into prison.

That night the Grand Inquisitor, an old man who has served the church throughout his long life, visits Christ in the dungeons and talks with him. It is in fact a monologue, because Christ remains silent throughout. The Grand Inquisitor tells Christ that he will have him burned at the stake the next day as the worst of heretics, because he has come back to undo the work of the church. The point is that the Grand Inquisitor understands perfectly that Christ came to offer freedom to humanity: he wanted humanity's free, unforced love, in place of the ancient rigid law. This lies at the heart of the temptation scene in the desert: if Christ had agreed to turn stones into bread, he would have had no difficulty in persuading people to follow him—people everywhere would have flocked to him. But Christ rejected that option—he resisted the temptation. He refused to coerce humanity, he didn't want blind obedience. He preferred freedom.

But, says the Grand Inquisitor, that was a mistake. Humanity doesn't want freedom, humanity simply wants to be happy. And the only way to make humanity happy is deprive humanity of freedom. Humanity's greatest need is to find someone [responsible] to whom they can hand over their gift of freedom as quickly as possible, and that, says the Grand Inquisitor, is where the church stepped in. The church, not Christ, has humanity's happiness in mind. The church had the good sense to correct Christ's work, to take away humanity's freedom, to give humanity someone [responsible] to obey, and to provide them with the bread they asked for.

Throughout this monologue Christ remains silent. When the Grand Inquisitor has finished he waits for a reply. He longs for Christ to say something, however bitter, however terrible. But Christ says nothing. Suddenly Christ gets up and comes over to the old man and softly kisses him on his bloodless lips. That is all his answer.

The old man shudders. He goes to the door, opens it, and says to the Prisoner: 'Go, and come no more'. He lets him out, and the Prisoner goes away, disappearing into the dark alleys of the town.[52]

Cameron asserts that the Grand Inquisitor is a very good example of the kind of Christians who would take the responsibility on themselves to make sure they put people like him on trial for heresy. 'The only uncharacteristic thing about the Grand Inquisitor is that he is fully conscious of the implications of his philosophy: he actually intends to correct the work of Christ, to rewrite Christianity.' Most Christians, he says, try to 'persuade themseves' that, in rewriting Christianity, they are somehow 'imitating Christ'. But, that apart, he says, the Grand Inquisitor is a great example that 'illustrates perfectly' the Christians that we are up against, who have

> a fear of freedom; a belief in the importance of controlling what people believe; a corresponding preference for obedience rather than love; a desire to give people what they want rather than the truth; a refusal to allow themselves to be in the least disconcerted when they are confronted with the true nature of their religion; and a readiness to persecute anyone who is of a different persuasion.[53]

The final verdict: a tragic irony, a terrible pity, and a veritable catastrophe

'What a pity,' Annie Dillard exclaims, with some degree of exasperation, 'that so hard on the heels of Christ come the Christians!'[54]

'Christianity is the very opposite of the revelation of God in Jesus Christ,' declares an obviously deeply distressed Jacques Ellul.[55] Wilhelm Reich asks the question:

> Can you imagine Christ riding a fiery white stallion ahead of a column of mounted Maccabeans, with sword drawn, blinking in the early morning sun and shouting 'Heigh! Ho! Forward Charge!'? It is unthinkable, impossible, perfectly ridiculous. You can imagine Caesar, Napoleon, Hitler, but not Christ. Christ simply does not fit.[56]

Ellul claims, 'In fabricating Christianity [with such a triumphalistic Christ] Christians have forsaken the Lord!' And for what? 'For human aggrandisement and nothing else!' [57]

When did this fabrication first take place? Reich says it was all Paul's fault. 'Paul is to Christ what Stalin is to Marx!' he says.[58] Ellul says, not at all! It's not Paul's fault, but ours. Whenever we are afraid to embrace the radical practice of faith and freedom to which both Christ and Paul have called us, and 'for whom [the] practice is the touchstone of authenticity,' he says, we betray 'both Christ and Paul'.[59]

Probably the most infamous, definitive betrayal in the history of Christianity was when the beleaguered followers of Christ bartered their faith and freedom, for the state subsidy and security that Constantine offered them. 'Through the Edict of Milan, which legalised the new religion in 313,' Thomas Cahill asserts, 'Christianity [was] received into Rome, not Rome into Christianity, [and was] made into the emperor's pet!'[60] Christ, who had turned the Roman Empire upside down, was turned into a lapdog for the Roman Emperor. According to A.N. Wilson, the Nicene Creed, to which all Christians now subscribed on pain of banishment, notably 'contained not one jot of the ethical teachings that Jesus had once preached.'[61]

Not for the Emperor, a Jesus who called upon his followers to 'love your enemies, love them, not hate them, bless them, not curse them, turn the other cheek, and take up your cross and follow me'; but the 'unthinkable, impossible, perfectly ridiculous', imperial Christ 'riding a fiery white stallion ahead of a column of mounted Maccabeans, with sword drawn, blinking in the early morning sun and shouting "Heigh! Ho! Forward Charge!"'

From that time onwards, no-one on Christian territory has been safe from Christian tyranny imposed in the name of an imperial

Christ. Jacques Ellul laments the fact that 'freedom finds little place in church history.' He says ' if one turns to history'—as we have—'it is surely apparent that Christians have more often imposed restraints, than championed liberty.' He says, as we have witnessed for ourselves, that 'whenever the church has been in a position of power, it has regarded freedom as an enemy.' And he sadly concludes that Christianity 'has been a veritable catastrophe!'[62] Hence, if it is true that, in Paul's quaint turn of phrase, 'for freedom Christ has set us free,' then one might have to say, with the 'heretic' Peter Cameron, that 'Christian freedom means freedom from Christianity!'[63]

Christianity is Dead: Long Live Christi-Anarchy!

'The indictment of Christianity is just.'[1] So says Wendell Berry, a farmer and writer, and according to the *New York Review of Books*, 'perhaps the great moral essayist of our day'. Berry, an American Christian, says that

> the complicity of Christian priests, preachers, and missionaries in the cultural destruction and economic exploitation of the primary peoples ... [of the Americas] is notorious. Throughout the five hundred years since Columbus's first landfall in the Bahamas, the evangelist has walked beside the conqueror. [Evangelical] Christian organisations, to this day, remain indifferent to the rape and plunder of the world ... The certified Christian seems just as likely as anyone to join the military-industrial conspiracy to murder Creation![2]

What can we, 'whose native religion, for better or worse, is Christianity', do about it? asks Berry. 'We can turn away from it, or against it ... But ... a better possibility ... is that this, our native religion, should renew itself so that it may become as truly instructive as we need it to be'. For 'on such renewal of the Christian religion', now the dominant religion of our day, 'may depend the survival of the Creation'. [3]

Berry suggests that such renewal of the Christian religion may come from the anarchistic Christian tradition, which has always existed parallel to, and in implacable opposition to, the imperial Christian tradition, and which in practice 'is a correction equally of people, [popes], and kings'.[4]

Berry echoes the philosopher, Alfred North Whitehead. Whitehead says that we desperately need to rediscover the anarchistic Christian tradition, which predates the imperial Christian tradition.

> When the world accepted Christianity, Caesar conquered. The Church gave unto God the attributes that belonged exclusively to Caesar. The brief Galilean ministry of humility flickered throughout the ages uncertainly. There is however in the Galilean origin of Christianity another suggestion which does not emphasise the ruling Caesar, or the unmoved mover, or the ruthless moralist. A kingdom, not of this world, it dwells upon the tender elements of the world, which slowly, and in quietness, operate by love.[5]

As far as I am concerned, it is only by rediscovering such a tender spiritual tradition that we have any hope of saving ourselves from the consequences of the triumphalism that is killing us. Jacques Ellul, the late professor of law and sociology at the University of Bordeaux, called this tender anarchistic Christian tradition, 'X', to distinguish it clearly from the triumphalistic imperial Christian tradition which we have come to know as 'Christianity.'[6] I call it 'Christi-Anarchy'.

Now I know that to many Christians the word 'anarchist' is basically a synonym for the Antichrist. In fact, one of the most recent popular contemporary translations of the Bible, called *The Message*, actually refers to the Antichrist as the 'Anarchist'. Beware 'the Anarchist', it says, according to Eugene Peterson. 'He'll defy [God], and then take over every so-called altar. Having cleared away the opposition, he'll set himself up in God's Temple as "God Almighty".'⁷ Given that kind of press—in the Bible, no less—it's easy to understand why so many Christians would consider the anarchist their arch-enemy. However, such a profound misconception, and fundamental misrepresentation, of anarchy should not surprise us. For it is in the vested interest of the hierarchies of both church and state, whose very authority the anarchist contests, to depict the anarchist as the Antichrist. But it betrays any real desire to come to a true understanding of the dynamic relationship that exists between Christ and anarchy.

Certainly there are anarchists that are opposed to Christ. But there are also anarchists that are very passionate supporters of Christ. In fact, there have been many anarchists for whom Christ was the principal inspiration for their anarchy. From Tertullian (at first) through to Francis of Assisi; from John Wycliffe to Gerrard Winstanley; from Menno Simons to Søren Kirkegaard and Christoph Blumhardt; from Leo Tolstoy to Toyohiko Kagawa; from Peter Maurin and Dorothy Day through to Jacques Ellul and Vernard Eller. For all these people Jesus Christ was the supreme example of authentic anarchy—the creative nonviolent anarchist par excellence, working not from the top down, but from the bottom up, with the poorest of the poor, to empower people and enable them to realise their potential, as men and women made in the image of God.

This is the essence of Christi-Anarchy. And in my experience, Christi-Anarchy is as different from Christianity as day is from night, light is from dark, warmth is from cold, and having a nice quiet chat over a cup of tea with some friends, is from being thrown

out of your house into the street, with nowhere to go, and no-one
to go with you.

The dominant paradigm:
Closed-Set Christianity

There are two completely different paradigms that people through
the centuries have used to try to understand their relationship with
Christ. By far the most influential perspective is what I call the
Closed-Set Perspective adopted by Christianity (Figure 5).

According to the Closed-Set Perspective, a set is defined by its
enclosure. From this perspective, a set of people who claim to have
some connection to Christ, can be shown to be part of the set, by
ascertaining whether their
beliefs and behaviours are
within certain set
boundaries.

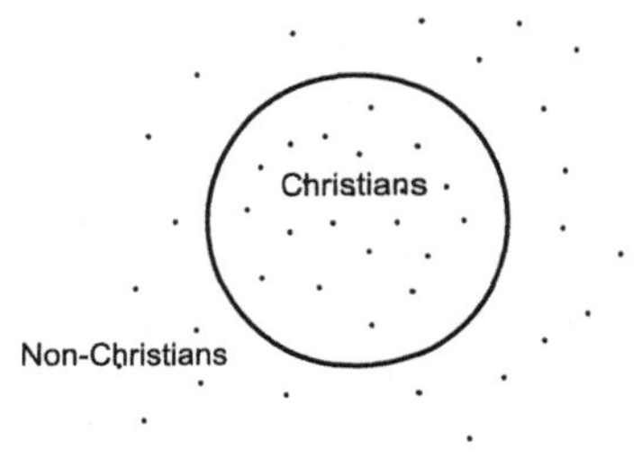

People can be part of
the 'in-set' by subscribing
to a certain set of
circumscribed beliefs and
behaviours, such as,
'confessing "Jesus Christ is
Lord",' and 'repenting of
their sins'. They then
become 'insiders'. People
who don't conform to the
set terms are not, and can
never be, a part of the in-
set. They are not insiders,
but 'outsiders'. If an

Figure 5: The Closed Set

Christians ·

Non-Christians

outsider is outside the set, but wants to become an insider, the only way for them to do so is by subscribing to the set terms. This is known as 'evangelism'. If an outsider is inside the set, but doesn't want to subscribe to the set terms, they will be put out. This is known as 'excommunication'.

It is through defending these boundaries of belief and behaviour that Christians define their identity as 'Christ-ians', or 'Christ's-ones'. Hence Christians tend to fight to the death to defend these boundaries of belief and behaviour. Not only their religious identity, but also their eternal destiny with Christ, depend on it.

There are certain obvious advantages that this Closed-Set Perspective affords Christianity. It is simple, precise, and portable; clear, concise, and communicable. The unconverted know what they have to do to be saved, and the converted know what they have to do to save others. And when everyone has done what they know has to be done, everyone can be sure they are saved. It is a dream come true for proselytisers—be they soap-box preachers, street-corner pamphleteers or super-duper televangelists. If you're a non-Christian you're out. If you're a Christian you're in. If you are out, and want to be in, just become a Christian. To become a Christian all you have to do is confess 'Jesus Christ is Lord' and repent of your sins. Once you're a Christian, you're in. And once you're in, you're in. Saved! Secure, safe and sound, forever—as long as you don't try to open up a discussion about the nature of the closed set itself, or to challenge the power of those who set the terms for the inclusion and exclusion of others.

Now the advantages of the Closed-Set Perspective are obvious to all those that are into Christianity quite uncritically. However its disadvantages are more obvious to those who relate to Christianity more analytically. To be sure it is straightforward, but it is also superficial. It is essentially static, unchanging, and

57

unchangeable. It is a homogeneous ideology that admits no questions, unless of course it asks and answers the questions itself. It is a uniform theology that demands complete conformity. There is no room at all for diversity, dissent or disagreement. It is reductionist: it reduces a relationship to Christ to a formula. It is exclusive, excluding anyone who cannot affirm the formula.

Is it violent? Not necessarily: but normally, for three reasons. Firstly, Christians tend to defend their boundaries to the death. Secondly, the best form of defence has always been attack. Thirdly, there are plenty of competing groups fighting for the right to define and defend their boundaries of belief and behaviour for themselves. Thus the Closed-Set Perspective rips the heart out of Christianity, replacing the warm, kind-hearted compassion of Christ with cold, hard-headed propositions about Christ, and relating to people in terms of an ideology of Christianity, rather than the love of Christ.

Many contemporary Christians are only too aware of the dreadful fallout associated with this Closed-Set Perspective. Paul Hiebert, Professor of Anthropology at Fuller Theological Seminary, raised the alarm in 1978, about the dangerous implications of what he called Bounded Set Christianity, in his seminal article on 'Conversion, Culture, and Cognitive Categories'.[8] What happens, Hiebert asks, if we define "Christian" in terms of a "Bounded Set"?

First, he says, we tend to distort the meaning of what it means to be a 'Christ-ian' or 'Christ-one'. Being a Christ-ian or Christ-one is essentially a matter of the heart. But 'because we cannot see into the hearts of people', we make a working definition, based on what 'we can see or hear—namely tests of orthodoxy [right beliefs], or orthopraxy [right behaviour]'. So we make our working definition for being a Christ-ian or Christ-one, essentially a heartless one.

Second, we tend to distort our understanding of the relationship between 'Christ-ians', and 'Non-Christians'. The two categories of people are 'sharply differentiated'. Because 'to have an unclear boundary is to undermine the very concept of "Christian" itself.' So we have one set of 'Christ-ians', who, by definition, are 'Christ's-ones'; and another set of 'Non-Christians', who, by definition, are 'Not-Christ's-ones'. There is no place for anyone, or anything, in between, not even Christ: only a well-defined, well-defended boundary.[9]

The theologian Robert Brinsmead comments on the serious consequences of maintaining the boundaries Paul Hiebert talks about.

Religion draws lines of demarcation through the human race. The chosen people are distinguished from the unchosen, insiders from outsiders, clean from unclean, believers from unbelievers, the enlightened from the unenlightened. People who live within separate barriers cannot effectively communicate. What is orthodoxy to one group, is blasphemy to other, and vice versa. (Take the deity of Christ for example. To Christians it is orthodoxy. To Muslims it is blasphemy.) Each religion produces an elite that regards itself as superior to the rest of humanity by virtue of possessing the truth. Such arrogance breeds estrangement and, eventually, hostility.

Bertrand Russell rightly states: 'Any average selection of humanity, set apart and told that it excels the rest in virtue, must tend to sink below the average.' When we observe the inhuman havoc caused by zeal for God, we must not naively think that it is only a result of the false religion, and that the anwer lies in finding the true religion.

The more people are nourished by their conceit over having the true religion, the more arrogant, authoritarian, and inhuman they become. The most dangerous human leaders are those who are least agnostic concerning the will of God and the most dogmatic about fulfilling his purpose. By its very nature, the relationship with a higher good than humanity is inevitably a relationship with a nonhuman belief that results in inhuman behaviour. Concrete examples of the ill-treatment of humanity, which inevitably follows such a devotion to religion are legion!'[10]

Brinsmead begs us to recognise that it is religious devotees such as ourselves, devoted to our various, mutually exclusive, inevitably conflictual, collision-bound Bounded Sets, that are directly or indirectly 'moving millions towards a jihad of violence everywhere' from Ireland to Lebanon, and from Bosnia to India.[11]

Stanley Hauerwas, Professor of Theological Ethics at the Divinity School, Duke University, struggles as a Christian with the whole notion that violence may be intrinsic to Christianity as we have conceived it. In reading the writings of Tyvetan Todorov, particularly *The Conquest of America*, Hauerwas says that he was brought face to face with the terrifying violence associated with the Christianization of his beloved Americas.[12] Todorov cites the example of Pedro de Alvarados, 'killing, ravaging, burning, robbing, and destroying all [over] the country ... wherever he came ... [in order] to subject ... [Native Americans] to the yoke and obedience of the church'. Hauerwas is naturally horrified by the cruelty, and recoils from the claim that such atrocities can be committed with a clear conscience in the name of Christ.

Todorov then cites the example of Bartolomé de las Casas, a contemporary of Pedro de Alvarados, criticizing Alvarados for his 'inhuman, unjust, and cruel' behaviour, 'because de las Casas is a Christian', and 'he loves Native Americans precisely because he is a Christian'. Here the name of Christ is not associated with support for atrocities, but with opposition to them. You can imagine Hauerwas, who has been holding his breath up to this time, starting to breathe a sigh of relief. Then, when he least expects it, Todorov throws Hauerwas a quick comment, followed by a big question, that hits him right where it hurts. He says that while de las Casas 'rejects violence' at a personal level, like most Christians, he is still more than willing when push comes to shove, to 'practise violence' at a political level. 'Is there not already a violence in the conviction that one possesses the truth oneself, and that one must further impose that truth on others?'[13]

Hauerwas struggles to answer this question the best he can, saying something about the need for Christians to be committed to persuasion rather than coercion in the process of conversion: which is a very important point, but doesn't answer the question. One of Professor Hauerwas's students makes this point in a letter he sends to his teacher, and that Hauerwas has the humility to print, as a counterpoint, in the back of his own book:

'Dear Professor Hauerwas,
    It seems to me, you have identified the crucial questions. When quoting Todorov you say 'Is there not already a violence in the conviction that one possesses the truth oneself, and that one must further impose that truth on others?' Later on you say, 'How can we communicate the gospel without explicitly or implicitly underwriting patterns of violence antithetical to Christ?' But you do not do justice to the questions you have raised. For all its merit, your solution of witnessing, (using persuasion, rather than coercion, to secure a conversion to your religion) does not engage the full weight of the questions you have raised—and for this reason: 'Is there not already violence implicit in the conviction that one possesses the truth oneself,

and that one must further impose that truth on others?' Whatever means one chooses to use to do so! Reread the long quote [you make] from Lesslie Newbigin, and imagine you are a Native American: 'As Newbigin reminds us, Christians can never seek refuge in a ghetto where their faith is not proclaimed as public truth for all. They can never agree that there is one law for themselves and another for the world. They can never admit that there are areas of human life where the writ of Christ does not run. They can never accept that there are orders of creation that exist otherwise than to serve Christ. The church can never accept the thesis ... that there has been no public revelation before the eyes of all the world of the purpose for which all people have been created ... The only possible product of that ideal is a pagan society.'

This is incredibly violent language, which has the rhetorical power of conveying that Christians should never accept the other [as the other], unless the other [becomes] one of the all [that are to be subject to Christianity]. It labels Native Americans as pagans (pejoratively construed), and excludes them, as they always have been, [from any knowledge of the truth].

Perhaps Christians should learn to shut up. I know this is no easy notion to work through, given the internal mechanisms [of the Closed-Set Perspective of Christianity] which drives the Christian to proclaim the news [the way they do], and yet it is *precisely* this proclamation which descends with such violence. I hope that you find at least some of my comments constructive. Peace, David Toole'.[14]

Hauerwas says that the letter is a reminder that our language 'can embody violence in ways that we hardly knew.' Certainly there are many Christians, like Hauerwas, who would be horrified to realise just how much the language of Closed-Set Christianity can, and does, embody violence towards anybody outside the boundaries of the Bounded Set. But unfortunately it is true. If we want it to be otherwise, we need to find another way of defining our faith that is not so defensive; another way of affirming our faith that is not so aggressive; a way of comprehending our faith that is true, but doesn't pretend to have a monopoly on truth; and a way of interpreting our faith that is inclusive, not exclusive, of all that is good and healthy and holy and right in other cultures, traditions and religions. And we can only do that if we scrap Closed-Set Christianity and consider the alternative: Centred-Set Christi-Anarchy.

The alternative paradigm:
Centred-Set Christi-Anarchy

The Centred-Set Perspective, adopted by Christi-Anarchy, is the exact opposite of the Closed-Set Perspective, adopted by Christianity (Figure 6).

According to the Closed-Set Perspective, a set is defined by an enclosure circumscribed by experts. According to the Centred-Set Perspective, a set is defined by a centre, which is free, and can never be enclosed, least of all by the experts. From this perspective, a set of people who have a connection to Christ show they are part of the set not by choosing to subscribe to a certain set of beliefs and behaviours within certain set boundaries, but by choosing to overcome any boundary of belief or behaviour that might prevent them from moving towards the free, beautiful, compassionate spirit of Christ, which they have made the centre of their lives. The essence of Closed-Set Christianity is all about being a 'Christian'— defining and defending being a 'Christ-ian'. The essence of Centred-Set Christi-Anarchy is all about becoming 'Christ-like' and encouraging everyone to become Christ-like, whether they become 'Christ-ians', or not.

Conversion in Closed-Set Christianity means confessing 'Jesus Christ is Lord', repenting of a prescribed set of sins, and, depending on the denomination involved, being baptised in water and/or the Holy Spirit.. Conversion in Centred-Set Christi-Anarchy means turning towards Christ, whether we know him by that name, or not, beginning to judge our own lives for ourselves, in the light of his love, and beginning to trust his love to sustain us on the journey of personal growth and social change that he is calling us to make.

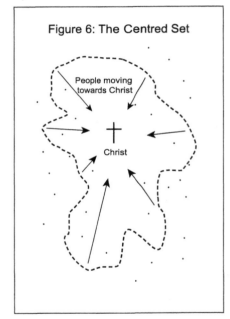

Figure 6: The Centred Set

There are some obvious disadvantages associated with the Centred-Set Perspective of Christi-Anarchy. What you see depends on where you stand, so different groups tend to see different disadvantages. Some of my non-Christian friends might say, 'Oh no, not Christ again. Christi-Anarchy sounds too much like Christianity to me. Won't you Christians ever give up trying to take over the world, one way or another!' Some of my Christian friends might say, 'Oh no, it's not really very Christian. There are no absolutes. It's all relative. Sure there are Christian words. But there are no Christian values.

It's all just vague, fluffy, feel good stuff—sugar and spice and all things nice. But it's got nothing to do with Christianity at all.'

Actually, I must admit, it can get quite confusing. A couple of years back I found myself in a situation where some of my non-Christian friends in the department of social work at the University of Queensland were accusing me of using social work language to promote Christianity, and, at the very same time, some of my Christian friends in the missions department at the Bible College of Queensland were accusing me of using Christian language to promote social work. My non-Christian friends were saying that the trouble was that I *was* a Christian; while my Christian friends were saying that the trouble was that I *wasn't* a Christian.

Which brings us to the major disadvantage of the Centred Set, as compared to the Closed Set. With a Closed Perspective it's easy to judge where people stand in relation to the set, who's 'in', and who's 'out'; whereas with a Centred-Set Perspective it is difficult, if not impossible, for anyone apart from Christ to judge whether anyone except themselves is 'in' or 'out'. Everyone in a Centred Set is moving towards the centre from a different angle, a different distance, and a different direction; and those that may be 'in', according to the Closed-Set Perspective, may be 'out'; and those that may be 'out', according to the Closed-Set Perspective, may be 'in'.

Take for instance the example of the enigmatic Tony Benn. Tony Benn was once Anthony Wedgwood Benn, Lord Stansgate. But he says he went through some kind of conversion, gave up his title, and joined the left wing of the British Labour Party to fight for equality for all. Recently a friend of mine, Simon Mayo, interviewed Tony Benn for 'The Big Holy One', an irreverent religious programme on the B.B.C. In the course of the interview Simon said to Tony, 'I hear that you have a faith of some kind. Would you like to tell us about it?' 'I believe in Christ.' replied Tony. 'Ah!' said

Simon, rather mischieviously. 'But is he your Lord?' 'Is he my Lord? Is he my Lord?' said Tony, aghast at the inanity of the question. 'Of course he's not my Lord. I don't believe in Lords. If I believed in Lords I'd still be one myself.' By this time most Christians would have turned off. At the very least they would have written off Tony's claim to faith, as he didn't even pass the most elementary test of authenticity. But Simon knew better. He gave Tony the opportunity to explain his faith for himself, in his own words. 'So,' said Simon, 'If you can't relate to Christ as your Lord, how do you relate to him?' As quick as a flash, the old trade unionist said, 'Well, he's more like my shop steward, I suppose. My trade union organiser!'

According to the Closed-Set Perspective Tony is definitely 'out'. But according to the Centred-Set Perspective Tony may actually be 'in'. And those that would say he is 'out' may actually be 'out' themselves. Now this kind of fuzzy logic drives Christians crazy. So to deal with the fuzziness of the fuzzy set, Christians have tried to incorporate Centred-Set Christi-Anarchy, as a subset, into Closed-Set Christianity (Diagram 7).

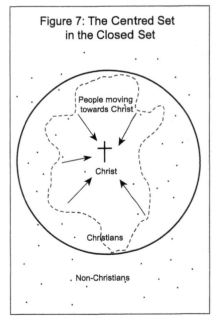

Figure 7: The Centred Set in the Closed Set

People moving towards Christ

Christ

Christians

Non-Christians

Jim Peterson says, 'It is not that Bounded Sets are bad, and Centred Sets are good. Discipleship is a Centred Set. To be a disciple is to be constantly moving toward the centre, which is Christ. [But] salvation is a

Bounded Set. Boundaries do exist. There is a boundary that sets the standard. One is either in Christ, or not in Christ.'[15] Now this solution, of defining 'salvation' as a 'Bounded Set', and 'discipleship' as a 'Centred Set', certainly solves the problems of confusion. With 'Closed Set' criteria it is always easy to determine who is 'in' and who is 'out'.

However, there are many problems with this solution. The first problem I have with Peterson's point of view is that it shows a fundamental misunderstanding of the relationship between salvation and discipleship. Peterson assumes salvation is separate from discipleship, and comes prior to discipleship; whereas the Gospels show that salvation, being saved, depends on discipleship, choosing to follow in the footsteps of the Saviour. Jesus said, 'Not everyone who says to me, "Lord, Lord," will enter into heaven, but only those who do the will of my Father who is in heaven.' (Matthew 7:21) 'Follow me.' (Matthew 9:9) 'If anyone would come after me, let them deny themselves, and take up their cross.' (Matthew 16:24) 'Those who endure to the end will be saved.' (Matthew 10:22)

The second problem I have with Peterson's point of view is that it shows a fundamental misunderstanding of the relationship between salvation and discipleship, and boundaries and sets. Peterson assumes that the only way to have a boundary between 'not being saved' and 'being saved' is by having a set boundary. Thus salvation can only be understood in terms of a Bounded Set. However, though there are no set boundaries in the Centred Set, there are still boundaries. And one crosses the boundary from 'not being saved' to 'being saved', by choosing to follow in the footsteps of the Saviour. In the Bounded Set the boundary is 'set' in the same place for everyone, no matter where they are coming from. In the Centred Set the boundary is moving all the time to accommodate anyone who makes a move towards the centre, whether they cross a set boundary, or not.

The Gospels show that 'being saved' depends on 'choosing to follow in the footsteps of the Saviour,' but that may mean different paths for different people, depending on where they are coming from. Christ called everyone to follow in his footsteps. But he expected one person to *leave* home (Matthew 8:22), while on another occasion he expected a person to *go* home (Mark 5:19). His expectations of them were exactly opposite, based on their personal circumstances at that particular time and place. Christ challenged everyone to give generously to the poor. But he expected one person to sell *all* that he had to give to the poor (Mark 10:21) and another person to sell only *half* of what he had (Luke 19:8–10). His expectations were not set standards, but individual variations on a common theme.

This brings us to the third problem I have with Peterson's point of view. It shows a fundamental misunderstanding of the Gospels. The perspective presented in the Gospels is not a Bounded-Set Perspective. Christ came to set people free from bondage to the Bounded Set. He did not want to be bound, and he did not want anybody else to be bound, by the boundaries of a Bounded Set. 'The boundaries are made for us, not us for the boundaries,' he once said, much to the consternation of the devotees of the Sabbath Sect Bounded Set (Mark 2:27). He bent the rules. He broke the regulations. He encouraged others to do likewise. 'Why don't you judge for youselves what is right?' he said (Matthew 12:57). 'You shall know the truth, and the truth will set you free!' (John 8:32)

For all its difficulties, the perspective presented in the Gospels is not a neat and tidy, domesticated, and domesticating, Closed-Set Perspective, but a warm and fuzzy, liberated, and liberating, 'Centred-Set Perspective' (Figure 8). There are many advantages that the Centred-Set Perspective affords Christi-Anarchy. The first advantage is that it is centred. Stanley Jones, the famous inter-faith evangelist, says, 'Get the centre right, and the circumference takes care of itself.'[16] The second advantage is that it is centred on Christ. Jones says that Christ is 'the Best to which all Good points',[17] but that 'Christianity has become ec-centric, off centre, away from Christ.' The world has too much Christianity, and too little Christ. Christi-Anarchy at least seeks to be 'Christ-centred.'[18]

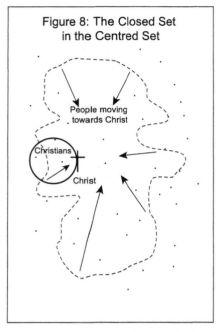

Figure 8: The Closed Set in the Centred Set

People moving towards Christ

Christians

Christ

The third advantage is that as we move towards the centre, Christ, we can move beyond the scriptures, creeds, rites, rituals, ceremonies, and even religions, that divide us, towards the One who can unite us as human beings made in the image of God. 'One, greater than the Bible, is here', Jones says.

> We love the Bible, honour it, assimilate it, for it leads us to his feet. But the Bible is not the revelation of God. It is the inspired record of the revelation. The revelation we have seen in the face of Jesus Christ. 'You search the scriptures, imagining you possess eternal life in their pages—and they do testify to me—but you refuse to come to me for life.' (John 5:39). Eternal life is not in the pages; it is in Christ who is uncovered through the pages.[19]

'One, greater than the creeds, is here,' Jones says.

> The creeds attempt to fix in statement what we see in Christ.
> We are grateful for these attempts—grateful, but not saisfied. A
> fixed creed becomes a false creed. Christ is ever beyond us
> calling us to new meanings. Hence our creeds must be eternally
> open to revision—revision toward larger, fuller meanings.[20]

One, greater than our rites, rituals, and ceremonies, is here, says
Jones. 'No rite, ritual, or ceremony of any kind is essential to
salvation. We are saved by Christ.'[21] One, even greater than our
faith, is here, Jones says. 'We sometimes say we are saved by faith.
That would make faith the means of our salvation. We are not saved
by faith, but by faith in Christ.'[22]

Christ is much greater than Christianity, Jones says. 'John said
to Jesus: "Master, we saw a man casting out demons in your name,
but we stopped him because he is not a follower of ours." Jesus said
to him "Do not stop him; he who is not against you is for
you."(Luke9: 49-50) John tried to make "in your name" and "a
follower of ours" synonymous. We still do that. Jesus showed the
difference. "He who is not against you is for you".' This is true
whether they are Christian or not.[23]

The fourth advantage is that as we move towards the centre,
Christ, we can move beyond the scriptures, creeds, rites, rituals
and ceremonies, and, even religions, that divide us, towards the
One who can unite us as human beings made in the image of God.
In *Jesus Before Christianity*, Albert Nolan writes:

> If we accept Jesus as our God, we would have to conclude that
> our God does not want to be served by us, he wants to serve us;
> he doesn't want to be given the highest possible status in our

society; he wants to take the lowest place, without any status; he does not want to be feared; he wants to be recognised in the sufferings of the poor; he is not supremely indifferent and detached, he is irrevocably committed to the liberation of humanity, for he has chosen to identify himself with all people in a spirit of solidarity and compassion. If this is not a true picture of God, then Jesus is not divine. If this is a true picture of God, then God is more truly human, more thoroughly humane, than any human being.He is a supremely 'Human God'. [24]

Robert Brinsmead then takes up the theme from Albert Nolan.

That is it! *A supremely human God!* When the Hebrew writers employed anthropomorphic expressions in referring to God, they were correct. They simply didn't go far enough. When God revealed himself in Jesus, he did not suddenly become human, he showed he always was supremely human. Was not the human made in his image? Because he is supremely human, Jesus in profound solidarity with the entire human race without distinction of race, colour, gender, culture, religion, or anything else. Wherever there is a human spirit, there is the God of compassion in solidarity with all suffering, loneliness and need. As with the great Hebrew prophets before him, the teachings of Jesus emphasised our inhumanity to one another. He taught that our duty to love humanity embraces everything and takes priority over everything. God is not absent here; but if he is loved, he is loved in and through humanity. Jesus himself says: 'So whatsoever you wish that people would do to you, do also to them; for this is the law and the prophets.' (Matthew 7:12)

'If you are offering your gift on the altar, and there remember that your brother or sister has something against you, leave your gift at the altar and go first and be reconciled to your brother and sister and then come and offer your gift.' (Matthew 5:23-24).

'And behold, one came up to him saying, "Teacher, what good must I do to inherit eternal life?" And he said to him, "If you would inherit eternal life keep the commandments." He said to him, "Which?" And Jesus said, "you shall not kill, you shall not steal, you shall not lie, you shall not commit adultery, you shall love your neighbour as yourself."' (Matthew 19:16-19)

Paul, the apostle of Jesus, says: 'Those who love their neighbour have fulfilled the law. For any other commandment is summed up in this sentence, "You shall love your neighbour as yourself".' (Romans 13:8-9) The light shining in the face of Jesus finally frees us from the dehumanising tyranny of devotion to a higher good than humanity. Humanity is the highest good. In this light we are at last free to be truly human in fulfil[ing] our duty. For our duty is this: 'You shall love your neighbour as yourself'.[25]

In both Christianity and Christi-Anarchy, Christ is the truth. In Christianity, people tend to think that, because Christ is the absolute truth, and they have a relationship with Christ, they know the truth absolutely. However in Christi-Anarchy, people tend to feel that while Christ is the absolute truth, and, through our relationship with Christ, we have a vision of the absolute truth, none of us has a monopoly on the truth.

In Christi-Anarchy there is a recognition that all of us are relating to Christ relatively, coming to Christ from different angles, different distances, and different directions, and hence that we know Christ only from the perspective from which we come.

In Christi-Anarchy there is, in fact, a recognition that we will only have the chance to know the truth completely when we come together with those who are approaching the truth from completely different, even contradictory, perspectives, to ourselves. So in Christi-Anarchy there is a realisation that any knowledge of the truth must ultimately be personal and relational and communal. As Parker Palmer says,

> When Jesus said, 'I am ... the truth', he did not say, 'I will tell you about the truth'; he claimed to embody the truth in his person. To those who wished to know the truth, Jesus did not offer propositions to be tested by logic in the laboratory. He offered himself, and his life. Those who sought truth were invited into relationship with him, and through him, with the whole community of the human and nonhuman world. When Jesus said, 'I am ... the truth', he was not making an idiosyncratic claim about a private individual, not inviting us into an isolated relationship that is either the whole of what we must know or separable from all the rest. Instead he was announcing and incarnating a new understanding of reality and our relationship to it. Truth is personal, to be known in personal relationships. The search for the truth becomes a quest for community with each other, and all creation.[26]

Through community with Christ we have a way of approaching truth without possessing it, and a way of interpreting truth that is inclusive, not exclusive, of all that is good and healthy and holy and right in other cultures, traditions and religions. Where Christianity defines faith in Christ in terms of boundaries of belief and behaviour that need to be defended, Christi-Anarchy defines faith in Christ in terms of a choice to overcome any boundary of belief or behaviour that might prevent us from moving towards the free, beautiful, compassionate spirit of Christ, which we have made the centre of our lives.

In Christianity the core issue of faith is defending the boundaries of the set—certain propositions about Christ which define the set. In Christi-Anarchy the core issue of faith is affirming the centre of the set, the person of Christ who defines the set. So, from this perspective, our role is *not* to defend certain propositions about Christ, *but* to affirm the person of Christ, by assisting one another to discern the presence of Christ in our lives, and then develop the capacity to process our lives—our cultures, our traditions, and our religions—in relation to the spirit of Christ. 'I realise that this interpretation of the personal truth of Jesus will not, at first glance, put non-Christians at ease.' says Parker Palmer. 'They will suspect me of trying to Christianise the universe, of wanting to put the whole of creation under a theological umbrella that leaves other spiritualities out in the rain ... Such people may understandably wish that I would put Jesus back in the box.'

'But', says Parker Palmer, persistently,

> by my view ... the personal truth of Jesus is not divisive and discriminatory. It is ultimately capacious. As Paul says, life in Christ breaks down all the cultural, [traditional, and religious] distinctions between us (Galatians 3:28). I am not arguing for a theology that aims at pushing or pulling all persons into doctrinal conformity. It is not necessary to accept Jesus as Lord in order to find in him a paradigm for personal truth. In him, truth, once understood as abstract, principled, propositional, suddenly takes on a human face and a human frame. Jesus, the disembodied "word" takes on flesh and walks among us. Jesus calls us to truth, but not in the form of world-views. His call to truth is a call to community—with him, with each other, with

creation and its Creator. Jesus stands against all...the threat[s] to community posed today by certain sectarian movements...not the least those committed in his name.[27]

Recently the Dalai Lama, the redoubtable Buddhist leader, said that 'for a Buddhist, when coming into contact with someone like Jesus Christ, the feeling that one would have would be that of reverence toward a fully enlightened being or bodhisatva.' During a special series of lectures he was giving on 'The Good Heart' of Jesus Christ, he said that, as far as he was concerned, the life of Christ 'clearly demonstrates...a way [of] bringing about liberation, and freedom from suffering...'[28]

Mahatma Gandhi suggested that if Christ could only be unchained from the shackles of Christianity, he would become 'The Way', not just for Christians, but for the whole world. 'The gentle figure of Christ, so patient, so kind, so loving, so full of forgiveness that he taught his followers not to retaliate when struck, but to turn the other cheek—was a beautiful example, I thought, of the perfect person.'[29]

He said he thought of Christ as 'a martyr, an embodiment of sacrifice', and of the cross as 'a great example of Jesus' suffering', and 'a factor in the composition of my underlying faith in nonviolence, which rules all my actions.'[30]

I refuse to believe that there exists a person who has not made use of his example, even though he or she may have done so without realising it ... The lives of all have, in some greater or lesser degree, been changed by his presence ... And because Jesus has the significance, and transcendency to which I have alluded, I believe he belongs not to Christianity, but to the entire world; to all people, it matters little what faith they profess.[31]

'Leave Christians alone for the moment', he said. 'I shall say to the Hindus that your lives will be incomplete unless you reverently study... Jesus.'[32] 'Jesus did not preach a new religion, but a new life,' said Gandhi-ji. 'Jesus lived and died in vain if he did not teach us to regulate the whole of life by the eternal law of love.'[33]

This is the challenge of Christi-Anarchy—to find a way to live 'the whole of life' in the light of 'the eternal law of love', embodied in the shining example of the person of Christ.

The Way of Christ:
the Way of Compassion

Our planet is in trouble. And religion, which was meant to make things better, often has made things worse. We suffer not for the want of religion, but for the want of love. If we are to have any hope of survival in the new millennium, we need to find a way to care for ourselves and for the world in which we live. *Compassion is not merely our best hope; it is our only hope.*

But how can this generation, that is more troubled than ever before—more disillusioned, more lonely, and more depressed; more anxious, more angry, and more aggressive—how can this generation rediscover the capacity to care enough to save us from destruction?[1] Especially when so often so many of us experience so little care ourselves in the increasingly dysfunctional families, disintegrating communities, and destructive political-economies that shape our lives?[2] Everywhere we turn, we are encouraged to opt, not for care, but for the slick, quick-fix kill, which doesn't bother about trying to solve problems, but simply blows them away.[3]

The psychologist, Dan Goleman, says that the question about the survival of humanity is a question that all of us will have to answer in our own hearts. He says that at the heart of the matter is empathy, the capacity for us to feel how others feel. He says, 'It is in empathising with potential victims—people in danger or distress—and feeling how they might feel [that we can be] motivated to refrain from harming them, and, hopefully, even perhaps consider helping them.[4] Empathy, Goleman says, is 'the basis of compassion'.[5]

The philosopher, John Macmurray, says that while most of us might be willing to give intellectual assent to the priority of rediscovering our capacity for empathy, it will not happen unless all of us give some emotional affirmation to that intellectual assent, and make it happen.[6] He says the issue is not so much a conflict between our heads and our hearts, but a conflict that we have in our hearts.[7] In our hearts, he says, we know that we cannot live without love, and that love involves an enhanced sensibility: an enhanced appreciation of, and affection for, one another's lives. But in our hearts, we also know that if we develop an enhanced sensibility towards the beautiful, yet painful reality of one another's lives, it will inevitably entail great agony as well as great joy. So we vacillate, wanting to become more loving, yet wanting to become anything but more loving, both at the same time.

As we prevaricate, we are tempted to withdraw from sensibility, which involves a greater sensitivity toward the total reality of one another's lives, into sentimentality. This involves more sensitivity to those parts of one another's lives which are less painful (like rumour, innuendo, scandal and trivia), and less sensitivity to those parts of one another's lives that are more painful (like disadvantage, disability, disease and death).[8] Thus we tend to retreat into an unreal world of infotainment, sitcoms, chat-shows, and hot-goss magazines, which give us the illusion of relating to the real world, but in fact do not relate to it at all.

But Macmurray reminds us that the only way we can live, is to live in the real world; the only way we can live in the real world, is to love the real world; and the only way we can love the real world, is to overcome our fear of the suffering that love in the real world involves. We must not allow that fear to so take over our lives that we put all our efforts into building up our defences against the world, and so alienate ourselves from the very reality to which we need to relate.

Macmurray says we must find a faith that can help us overcome our fear of the suffering, so that we can embrace the world as it is, love it, warts and all, and live our lives, with friend and foe alike, to the full.[9] The only way he knows, that we can do this, is by following the way of Christ.[10]

Jesus Christ: the archetype of compassion

I believe that Christ is the archetype of compassion: the original model of radical non-violent sacrificial love that humanity desperately needs, now more than ever, if it is to find a way to save itself from the cycles of violence that will otherwise destroy it.[11] As the famous analytical psychiatrist, Carl Jung, once said:

> One of the most shining examples that history has preserved for us is the life of Christ. Obeying the inner call of his vocation, Jesus voluntarily exposed himself to the assaults of imperial madness that filled everyone, conqueror, and conquered alike. In this way he recognised the nature of the psyche which had plunged the whole world into misery. Far from allowing himself to be suppressed by this psychic onslaught, he consciously assimilated it. Thus was a world-conquering Roman Empire transformed into the universal Kingdom of God. His religion of love was the exact psychological counterpoint to the politics of power. Jesus pointed humanity [to] the truth that where force rules there is no love, and where love reigns force does not count. [12]

As a recent survey in *Psychology Today* showed, it is to Jesus that most of us who know anything about him still feel we need to turn, if we are ever going to learn anything about love.[13]

Christ figures: other types of compassion

I believe that in every culture, tradition and religion, in every part of the world, there are types of Christ—Christ-like figures who, somehow or other, prefigure the spirit of Christ—to whom we can turn, and who in turn can point us towards the person of Christ himself.[14]

George Rosendale, a respected elder from Hopevale, an Aboriginal community in far north Queensland, says that in his culture the Christ figure was someone called the 'Maladikarra'.

> If someone is before the Aboriginal law court, and is condemned to die, the way he is to die is by being speared by his people. When he is to be speared, he has the right to get a defender. In my language we call him 'Maladikarra'. The Maladikarra 'speaks for the one that is in trouble.' If he cannot persuade the court to stop the spearing, then the Maladikarra stands in front of this other man, between him and the fifty or sixty people who are going to spear this man. The Maladikarra says to this man, 'All right, don't watch the people, don't watch the spears, only watch me. Watch my movements. Whichever way I move, you follow my actions.' They don't throw the spears one at a time. They throw them whenever they wish. Five or six spears come at one time. The Maladikarra stands has to stop these spears. He knocks the spears away with his woomera. He does this until all the spears are broken. When this is done, the man is free. The Maladikarra stakes his life to save this other man.[15]

'There is a tremendous message here,' says George. 'It is the message of Christ. He is the great Maladikarra.' [16]

In Buddhism, for many people the Christ figure would be the 'Bodhisattva'. A Bodhisattva literally means 'someone with heroic aspirations for true enlightenment', a compassionate person with the courage to forgo their own salvation in order to save others from suffering.[17]

'For me, as a Buddhist', says the Dalai Lama, 'my attitude towards Christ is that of reverence towards a Bodhisattva.'[18] The prayer of the Bodhisattva, one of the Dalai Lama's favourite prayers, is: 'as long as space abides, and as long as sentient beings remain, may I too abide, and dispel the suffering of sentient beings.'[19]

In Hinduism, for many people the Christ figure would be Krishna, at least the Krishna of the *Bhagavad Gita*, if not the Krishna of the *Mahabharata*. The Krishna in the *Bhagavad Gita* says that, 'whenever there is a failure of righteousness, an uprising of unrighteousness, then I create myself. For the establishment of righteousness I appear age after age.'[20]

Even though he was a warrior, fighting on the battlefield at the time that he said these words, for people like Mahatma Gandhi the Krishna of the *Bhagavad Gita* is still a model of radical non-violent sacrificial love because, he says, Krishna is mythological, the *Bhagavad Gita* is allegorical, and the fight to which we are called is a metaphorical battle, of love against hate.[21] 'Hinduism is based', Gandhi says, 'on the firm foundation of nonviolence'.[22] 'The religion of nonviolence', he says,

is not meant merely for the *rishis* or saints. It is meant for the common people as well ... Nonviolence is a power which can be wielded equally by all, provided they have a living faith in the God of Love, and therefore have an equal love for all mankind. I swear by nonviolence, because I know that it alone conduces to the highest good of mankind. I object to violence because, when it appears to do good, the good is only temporary, the evil it does is permanent ... Nonviolence works for the good of all, not only of the greatest number. The votary of nonviolence must be prepared, if necessary, to lay down his life for the good of all'.[23]

In Islam, for many people the Christ figure would be Mohammed, particularly the early Mohammed, especially during his time in Mecca. Badshah Khan says:

> There is nothing surprising in a Muslim like me subscribing to the creed of nonviolence. It is not a new creed. It was followed 1,400 years ago by the Prophet all the time he was in Mecca, and it has since been followed by all those who wanted to throw off an oppressor's yoke.[24]

Khan says that the true life of a Muslim is a life of nonviolence. 'It is my inmost conviction', he says, 'that Islam is *amal* or work, *yakeen* or faith, and *muhabat* or love, and without these the name Muslim is sounding brass and tinkling cymbal'.[25] Khan says to his detractors that 'if you read about our Prophet it becomes clear that he never used the sword as an instrument of *jihad* or holy war.'[26] *Sabr* or patience, he says, 'is the weapon of the Prophet. If you exercise patience, endure all hardships, victory (in the holy war between good and evil being waged in every human heart) will be yours'.[27]

Khan quotes the Koran as saying, 'there is no compulsion in religion',[28] 'forgive and be indulgent',[29] 'render not vain your almsgiving by injury,'[30] 'whosoever killeth one for other than manslaughter, it shall be as if he had killed all mankind, and whoso

saveth the life of one, it shall be as if he had saved the life of all
mankind.'[31]

In Judaism, for many people the Christ figure would be
Joseph. According to Elie Wiesel, 'Abraham is respected; Isaac is
pitied; Jacob is followed; but only Joseph is loved ... One loves
him more readily, more joyously than any other biblical figure
... Abraham was obedient; Isaac was brave; Jacob was faithful;
but only Joseph was just ... Joseph, and Joseph alone, among all
our ancestors ... [is called a] Tzaddik, a Just Person, an Example
of Righteousness'.[32]

Joseph was the eleventh of the twelve sons of Jacob. To the
aged father he was the dearest child. Joseph helped his brothers
tend the flocks in the fields. One day, when he was seventeen,
he turned up in a 'coat of many colours', which was a gift from
his father. The older brothers were jealous. And their jealousy
became hatred when he told them of the dreams he had, that
he would be a great ruler.

One day they got so sick of him that they took him, and sold
him to some passing traders as a slave. The brothers then killed a
goat, tore the coat, stained it with goat's blood, and brought it to
Jacob, saying Joseph had been killed by a wild animal.

Meanwhile Joseph was carried off to Egypt. Potiphar, the
captain of the palace guard, bought him. Joseph served his master
so well that he was made the overseer of Potiphar's household.
But Joseph offended Potiphar's wicked wife, because he would
not return her illicit love for him. Potiphar's wife had Joseph
thrown into prison. But Joseph won the jailer's confidence, and
was placed in charge of all the prisoners in the prison. Pharaoh's
butler had offended his lord, so he was put into prison with
Joseph too.

One night the butler had a strange dream. And Joseph interpreted the dream for him. Two years later, when the Pharaoh had a dream, the butler, now restored to the Pharaoh's favour, remembered Joseph's interpretation of his dream, and he recommended Joseph to the Pharaoh. Joseph told the Pharaoh that his dreams indicated that there would be seven years of good harvests followed by seven years of bad harvests, and that he needed to appoint an administrator to collect food in preparation for the coming famine. The Pharaoh appointed Joseph to the position.

During the famine, when his brothers came to Egypt to get some food supplies, they came face to face with Joseph, but they failed to recognise the Prime Minister. So Joseph made himself known to them. They were terrified, fearing his revenge. But Joseph gladly forgave them. And invited them to live with him. So the brothers went home, and brought their father and their families to live with Joseph in Egypt.[33]

'No wonder that in our traditional literature', writes Elie Wiesel, 'Joseph is an object of passionate admiration, bordering on worship.'

Here is a person who was indebted to no one, and that made him a free man; who owed his success only to his natural gifts; and, who through his use of his natural gifts transformed exile into a kingdom, misery into splendour, and even humiliation into mercy.[34]

'Here is our example,' he says. 'He assumed his destiny and tried to give it meaning from within. He lived his eternal life in the here and now, demonstrating that it is possible for a slave to be a prince, for the dreamer to link the past to the future, and for the victor to open himself to the supreme passion that is love.'[35]

Not all the people who are types of Christ are well-known leaders of world-renowned religions. In fact, most of them are not. Some of the most significant Christ figures in our lives may be ordinary, non-religious, even anti-religious, people who somehow—they may not even know how—at some moment represent something of the love of Christ to us. In my life there is a tough little Christ figure with thick glasses, spiky hair, and empty gums, who goes by the name of Dean.

Dean started his life behind the eight ball. A little kid, at the mercy of big merciless blokes, in an endless round of foster homes and special schools, Dean was knocked about a lot, and was constantly left feeling completely snookered. At the age of eighteen he was placed in a local hostel. I well remember meeting him, because at the time the only way Dean knew how to express his emotions was by thumping people, and he was apparently so glad to make my acquaintance that he almost killed me.

Since that time Dean and I have got to be quite good mates. We share a passion for Rugby League football, and are very passionate supporters of the Brisbane Broncos, who Dean and I reckon are probably the best Rugby League team in the world. We regularly go out together with a bunch of friends, to have a barbecue in a park down by the Brisbane River, and Dean has even been known, now and again, to drag me into a game of what we call 'touch footy'—a very fast, very skilful, non-contact training version of Rugby League that is really far too fast and far too skilful for an old fella like me, but it's a lot of fun.

As time has gone by Dean has, thankfully, learnt to express his love for his friends much more tenderly. He is now known more for his trademark quick chuckle, cheeky smile, and kindly touch, than for thumping people.

Not long ago, a brother-in-law of mine lapsed into an episode of psychotic despair, jumped off the Storey Bridge, which spans the Brisbane River, and tragically killed himself. Needless to say, I was devastated. When I told everybody at church how devastated I was, I noticed Dean, standing in the back of the room, listening intently to me. Before I realised it, he made his way to the front where I was standing, and stood beside me, with his arm around me, quietly waiting until I had finished what I was saying. Then all of a sudden, he gave me a huge hug, and said: 'Don't worry Dave. I'll be your brother-in-law.' I'll never forget that simple, unpretentious gesture of care. At that moment Dean represented the love of Christ to me.

The person of Christ: a passion for love and for justice

But Dean isn't Christ. He may point me to Christ, but Dean isn't Christ. God knows, he still even thumps me from time to time! It is to Christ, and to Christ alone, that all of us including Dean must turn, if we are going to learn the true nature of love and justice.

The political economy in which Jesus grew up was one of total captivity. Palestine was under the complete control of the Roman Empire, abetted as it was by prominent Jewish collaborators. The authorities levied taxes on the population that amounted to forty per cent of people's income, and their taxes were used to maintain the very army of occupation that the people despised. When revolts broke out from time to time, as the people tried to break free of the forces that controlled their lives, the Jewish collaborators aided the Roman rulers in putting down the rebellions. They cooperated with the very powers that oppressed their own people in order to maintain their position, their property and their monopoly of the market.

Not surprisingly, trade and commerce thrived under Pax Romana. The great Jewish Temple in Jerusalem became the symbol of that prosperity, combining the roles of stock exchange, central bank and government treasury. However Israel was still essentially an agrarian society: agriculture was not only the primary industry, but also the premier industry in society. Ownership of land was the main source of wealth. Most of the land was owned by a few rich families, who continued to acquire more and more land as the poor families were forced to sell land to pay the taxes that were imposed on them. Those poor people without any land at all, found themselves facing a very bleak future. They were forced to confront not only terrible financial insecurity, but also total fiscal vulnerability to the very system which dispossessed them in the first place. In this system the poor, the prisoners, the handicapped, the lepers, and other marginalised and disadvantaged people, literally had no one to help them. They were helpless.

One balmy Sabbath, at the very beginning of his ministry, Jesus visited the synagogue in his home town of Nazareth, and when he was asked to read a passage from the Holy Scriptures, he turned to a part written by the prophet Isaiah, which reads:

The Spirit of God has got hold of me,
    and is urging me to take on a special task;
to share good news with the poor,
    to free the prisoners,
    to help the handicapped,
and to smash the shackles of the oppressed ...
(Luke 4:18-19)

In so doing, Jesus announced in front of everyone that he knew at the time, that he wanted to make this heartfelt anarchistic manifesto his mission in life.

Jesus grew up with a passionate concern for the welfare of his people, especially those that no-one else particularly cared about. He was passionately concerned about the plight of the poor, the victims of the imperial system. He was passionately concerned about the predicament of the prisoners and the handicapped, excluded from all meaningful participation in society by bars of steel and stigma. He was passionately concerned about the condition of the lepers, not only because of the pain of their ulcers, but also because of the pain of their untouchability. And he was passionately concerned about the situation of ordinary people whose hope had all but been destroyed by their soul-destroying circumstances, and who consequently felt consigned forever to long days, and even longer nights of utter despair.

For Jesus, a passionate concern for people meant nothing less than a passionate commitment to them. He became forgetful of himself, living instead in constant remembrance of those around him who were themselves forgotten. He desperately wanted them to feel fully alive again, to revel once more in the joy of being loved, and being able to love. He worked tirelessly to set them free from all that might debilitate them, breaking the bonds of exclusivity, poverty, misery, and guilt. He welcomed the out-caste, helped the weak, healed the sick, and forgave the sinner, giving them all a chance of a new beginning. He didn't write anyone off himself, and he encouraged everyone that he met not to write one another off either. He challenged everyone to tear up their prejudices, trash their stereotypes, and get their act together—in-crowd and out-caste, strong and weak, rich and poor, saint and sinner—to support one another in the common quest for their own humanity.

Jesus was painfully aware of the captivity of the political economy in which he lived. He recognised that this captivity was perpetuated by preoccupation with power, position, and property, at the expense of people's lives. 'What the world esteems,' Jesus said, 'is disgusting to God!' (Luke 16:15)

His critique was universal, but Jesus actually chose to confront this captivity at a national, rather than an international level. Jesus was concerned more with the mechanisms of control perpetuated by his own people, than with the mechanisms perpetuated by others. For unless these indigenous mechanisms of control were dealt with, the foreign yoke might be thrown off, but the captivity would continue. So Jesus confronted the people in his own country—the people of his own culture, his own tradition and his own religion—with their responsibility for their own captivity, and for their own liberation.

'Don't judge others,' Jesus said. 'Judge yourself' (Matthew 7: 1-3). 'How sad it is', he said to them, that 'you neglect to do justice!' (Luke 11:42) 'What good will it do to gain the whole world and lose your own soul?' (Matthew 16:26)

His confrontation of captivity was at a national level, but Jesus actually chose to create the anarchistic communities that he advocated as the alternative, at the local rather than the national level. Jesus, the 'Lamb of God' (John 1:29), sought to develop his anarchistic communities, of what he called 'flocks of sheep' at the grass roots (John 10:11–16). 'Sheep' was a seemingly innocuous, but essentially subversive term that Jesus used to describe people who lived with 'wolves', but refused to become wolves themselves; even if it meant, as Jesus said it might, that the wolves might rip the 'flock' to pieces because of their refusal to join the 'pack' and prey on others.

'I want you to live your lives as sheep, even in the midst of wolves.' said Jesus. 'Be shrewd. But always be harmless' (Matthew

10:16). 'Always treat other people as you would like them to treat you,' he said (Matthew 7:12). 'Even do good to those who do evil to you. Love those who hate you. And bless those who curse you' (Matthew 5:44) 'Don't ever be afraid' he said to his flocks, 'of those who can kill the body, but cannot kill your soul.' (Matthew 10:28)

In his communities Jesus encouraged people to liberate themselves from the political economy, by developing compassion for people that transcended society's sick, obsessive, compulsive, preoccupation with power, position, and property. 'God is compassionate.' Jesus said. 'Be as compassionate as God.'(Luke 6:35–36)

In these counter-cultural communities Jesus encouraged people to consider other people to be of enormous importance: not just as producers or consumers, still less as subjects or objects, but as people in their own right. The people usually considered least important, and consequently pushed to the side, were treated as most important, and consequently given a place of respect. 'When you throw a party,' Jesus said, 'do not invite your friends, or your family, or your affluent neighbours. Invite those who have no friends, and those who have no family, and strangers who are anything but affluent.' (Luke 14:12–13)

All oppressive forms of politics were denounced. Charismatic leadership, based on experience, was expected to be exercised within a decision-making framework that functioned according to group consensus. 'We all know that bosses call the shots, and the heavies throw their weight around' said Jesus. 'But that's not the way we are going to operate. Whoever wants to be the leader of a group, should be the servant of the group' (Matthew 20:26)

All exploitative forms of economics were renounced. Generosity was expected to be exercised, and wealth freely shared, by the rich with the poor, in an earnest quest for genuine equality. 'Be on your guard against greed,' Jesus said (Luke 12:15). 'Give to anyone who asks. If anyone wants to borrow something, let them have it '(Matthew 5:42); 'lend without expecting anything in return' (Luke 6:35).

The anarchistic communities Jesus developed never smashed the political economy to which their society was captive. They never completely reconstructed the political economy in terms of the total liberation that they prayed for. But they did smash some of the mechanisms of control to which they were captive, and they did manage to reconstruct such a substantial degree of liberated, and liberating, alternative political and economic reality, that their experience has served as an example of true love and true justice ever since.

According to an eyewitness: 'They all met together, breaking bread in their homes and eating together with glad and jubilant hearts. They had everything in common, selling their possessions, and giving support to anyone who asked for help. So there wasn't a single person with an unmet need among them. And all the people spoke well of them.' (Acts 2: 44–47; 4: 32–35)

The experience of Christ: of compassion, of anguish and of struggle

The example of Christ is enormously powerful. It has profoundly challenged people, in each succeeding generation since the time of Christ, to be the very best that we as human beings can be. But his example is so powerful that many of us experience it as overpowering, and therefore unfortunately as disempowering, rather than empowering as it ought to be.

So we tend to treat Christ like our *idol,* someone that we'd like to be like, but know that we can never be like, rather than our *model,* someone that we'd like to be like, and do our best to emulate.

But Christ never wanted to be an idol. He never asked anyone to worship him. Christ only wanted to model how to live life to the full. All he asked of people who wanted to live this way, was to follow him.

To treat Christ as an idol—'the ideal to which we aspire, but not the reality we personify'—simply perpetuates Christianity and all its associated problems. The only way we can resolve these problems is by relating to Christ, not as a sacred idol, but as a role model, and, seeking not so much to be Christian, as to be Christ-like, as Christi-Anarchy suggests. But how can any of us ever be like Christ? This is a question we need to answer.

I think it's too much for any of us to expect to be Christ-like in terms of our *ability*. Very few of us, if any, could expect to be able to calm a storm, or raise the dead, as Christ did. But I think it's not too much for any of us to expect to be Christ-like in terms of our *sensibility*. Every single one of us should expect to be able to care for people, with compassion, as Christ did. And we can learn to be like Christ in that sense, only by following Christ, who will himself, he says, show us the way.

Christ doesn't merely *tell* us the way, he *is* the way. This is why Christi-Anarchy was originally simply known as 'The Way' (Acts 19:9). We can begin to follow the way of Christ even before we know it is the way of Christ—even before we know who Christ is—by following the way of Christ represented in the Christ figures we may have encountered along the way. But as we follow the way of Christ, we will get to know who Christ is, for Christ himself *is* 'The Way'.[36]

William Barclay, the beloved Scottish theologian, explains:

Suppose we are in a strange town and we ask for directions. Suppose the person says: 'take the first to the right, and the second to the left. Cross the square, and go past the church, and take the third on the right and the road you want is the fourth road on the left.' If that happens, the chances are we will get lost before we get half way. But suppose the person we ask says: 'Come. I'll take you there.' In that case that person is to us the way, and we cannot miss it. That is what Jesus does for us. He does not only give us advice. He takes us by the hand and leads us. He walks beside us, strengthens, and guides us, every day. He does not tell us the way; he is the way.[37]

If we want to know the way to live a life of compassion, Christ says to us: 'Come. I'll take you there.'

Vocation and temptation— and the Way of Christ

The other day I was speaking with a very enthusiastic young man. The conversation brought up a whole range of issues that have begun to concern me. There was no doubting this young man's sincerity, his resolve, or his passion for love and justice.

But, nonetheless, I became more and more anxious as the conversation continued. He seemed, if anything, too self-conscious about his sense of mission; too excited about the prospect of success; too scared about the possibility of failure; too determined to prove himself; too determined that he, and the people he was with, would save the world, damn it! He seemed prepared to do anything to make his dreams come true.

There was nothing, he seemed to suggest, that he was not prepared to do to accomplish his aspirations, no ploy that he was not prepared to try, no compromise that he was not prepared to make, in order to bring about the kind of world he believed our world ought to be. And, as I have said, this profoundly disturbed me.

I have met too many young men and women like this young man—good men and women with good ambitions, but haunted by doubts about their ability to bring about the kind of changes that they so desperately desire, and driven by the need to prove to themselves, and to others, that they have the capability required to accomplish such a significant task.

Too many of us are like this, tempted to be preoccupied with our own performance. We try very hard, striving strenuously to succeed. We do not sit easily with failure: our own, or anyone else's. Comparing ourselves with, and competing against others, we push ahead, and push people aside where necessary, in our desperate quest to save the world. Hence many of us who are most sincere are most insensitive. We, who are meant to be advocates of love and justice, often lack basic kindness, let alone the radical compassion that our world needs.

Many of us desire our mission to be effective; that it would make a significant difference to our world, perhaps even change the course of human history. We believe that we need to involve as many people as possible in our movement for change. We need to establish a popular base of support for our enterprise if we are going to bring about the change we envisage. In order to make our cause popular, we may be tempted to give people what they want, promising them some special privilege or some sensational experience in return for the promise of their support: colluding with their whims rather than challenging them to change their way of life. Hence many of us, who are supposed to be different, may not be much different from the status quo we are setting out to change.

Many of us desire the impact of our mission to be not merely a few ephemeral moments of exciting activity, but a meaningful durable accomplishment of lasting importance. In order to guarantee the long-term continuity of our project, we may find it necessary to forgo our original uncompromising approach, in favour of a more compliant attitude towards the power-brokers who hold the future of our programme in their hands. But in the process of negotiating support for our work, we may be tempted to sacrifice even the welfare of the very people that our work was originally intended to benefit, to ensure its survival. Certainly the people most likely to suffer most from top-level negotiations with key players, are the ordinary people at the bottom of the heap, who have no real bargaining power. Hence many of us who are supposed to be working for change, may end up selling out the poor that we are supposed to be working for, as so many people have done before.

We need to learn to deal with the temptations that come to us, as part of our struggle for love and for justice, the way Jesus did. We need to imagine how Jesus dealt with them, and live through his experience, so that we can learn to deal with them the way Jesus did. Picture the scene as it was for Jesus, when he came face to face with these temptations. 'Come.' says Jesus. 'I'll take you there.'

The scene is barren.
Jesus has journeyed into the wilderness
*   to a place the Jews call Jeshimmon,*
*   'the place of devastation.'*

He finds himself
*   amidst blasted hills and broken valleys,*
*   in a bare land strewn with hard boulders,*
*   where only the slow dust speaks.*

It is the ruin of a land;
*   the resting place of many a dream.*
Where the realities of life and death
*   take on stark contrasting shapes and colours.*

The desert's breath is stale and still,
   the air thick with the weariness of time.
It is a quiet place, without the confusion
   of a more so-called civilised situation.
Here he stops and sits and reflects,
   inhaling the quietness,
      listening to his heart.

This is a place of rumination;
   a place where the muddy water clears
      and the spirit plumbs its depths.

Jesus contemplates.

He thinks of his encounter with John,
   the man they call 'The Baptist'.

The skies tearing open,
   the fluttering of wings,
      the sound of the Voice.

A seeing and a hearing,
   a glimpsing of the unseen and the unspoken,
      a grasping of a vision and a vocation.

Earth and heaven bursting with a new beginning,
   and his own unbearable, undeniable, calling;

To hold the dream, and to not rest until it be born,
   to bear the pain of bringing it to birth.

He considers John.
  John, the prophet and the preacher,
    the wild man calling for wild changes.

Longing for the will of God,
  aching for love and justice in the land,
Insisting the impossible is possible,
  and not just possible, but imperative!

Jesus feels the echo of the message
  resounding in his own soul,
Smells the fragrance of the spirit
  wafting through the air.

Oh, to be a part of the movement;
  to bring the dream into being.
Fleshing out faith,
  speaking grace, practicing equality.

'Filling every valley, levelling every hill,
  making the crooked paths straight,
    making the rough paths smooth,
ensuring every man and woman
  knows the awesome salvation of God.'

Jesus feels his imagination soaring
  like an eagle in the empty sky.

And beneath it, far below it,
  the sobering landscape of reality.

Christi-Anarchy

How to bring heaven to earth
without destroying the synergy?

How to take a soul, grown bone weary,
and make it sing and dance again?

How to take a half-forgotten step,
and make it a wholehearted movement?

How to bring about genuine change in a world
where love is bought and sold,
justice goes to the highest bidder,
and freedom is a faint memory carried by the wind?

Unsummoned, the memory serves him a warning:
a roadside lined with impaled bodies on bloody crosses –
revolutionaries hung out, and left to dry,
for the treason of trying to fight for freedom.

Here, in the wilderness, without food or water,
Jesus waits and weighs up his options.

A thought comes to him—
'If you are who you claim to be,
if you have the potential
that you are supposed to have,
prove it!
That's it—just prove it!'
Then people will be with you.
And you will be unstoppable.'

Jesus turns his head and scans the horizon.
    There is nothing to see save the desert;
the wilderness scattered
        with boulders, rocks and stones.

And the thought comes to him—
    'If you turned these stones into bread
        then the masses would be behind you'.

Jesus remembers the masses
    gathering daily at dawn at the temple;
        waiting for the sunrise, and the signal
    from the priests in the tower, to begin a new day.

And the thought comes to him—
    'If you climbed that tower, and leapt down,
        and landed safely in the midst of that crowd,
    the masses would be with you all the way.'

Jesus remembers the masses
    of the twisted, tortured frames of the rebels
who had gone 'all the way' to change the world,
    but ended up hanging, ignominiously,
        on crosses at the side of the road
            like scarecrows in the sun.

Is this the fate of all dreamers and their dreams?
    Nailed to history as a lesson in futility?
        Are there no other options?
And the thought comes to him—

'If you were prepared to compromise,
accept the system, respect the status quo,
and work for change, gradually, incrementally,
then, maybe,
you could succeed, where others failed!'

Jesus feels these thoughts
worming their way into his heart.

And he begins to wrestle
with the issues that they raise.

Didn't he need to prove himself?

How else could he expect them to risk all
for a penniless carpenter from Nazareth?
Bet on an uneducated seer from Galilee
with nothing more than a pipe dream?

To ask a lot, you have to give a lot,
a sample, if you like, of what's possible.

It's only sensible.
Only reasonable. Only practical.

And what better way to show what's possible
than to provide the people
with more of the things that they want
and display your power in the process?

The Way of Christ

That would impress the people—wouldn't it?
That would ensure the support of the masses.
And that would mean a better deal,
when he came to terms with the system.

Jesus feels the rush of this logic
sweeping him inexorably downstream.

And he might have been carried away by it
except for a small stubborn rock of doubt.

How could a person, obsessed
with having to prove himself,
ever hope to lead a movement
dedicated to the service of others?

That would be impossible. Absolutely impossible.

So Jesus lets the wave of desire to prove himself
that is washing over him, simply come and go.

Where does that leave the idea of providing people
with the things that they wanted
and displaying his power, spectacularly, in the process?

Sure, it might assure him of support—but for what?
Spectacular events and free provisions!

And dishing out what people want
might distract them from what they need.

Bread and circuses may be fun
   but they don't bring transformation.
Miracles fade into memory,
   and bellies, once filled, are soon empty again.
Jesus knows full well
   the only way hungry people will be fed,
is if people create a culture of love and justice
   where they care, and share, with one another.

So.
   No side shows. No free lunches.

Where does that leave the idea of negotiating
   some kind of new deal with the system?

Jesus knows that, in the furnace of his soul,
   the answer to that question is already forged.
The middle ground is occupied territory,
   'negotiation' but another name for 'capitulation'.

Brokering some kind of deal with the system
   might provide him with safety and security himself.
But he knows that the system is always willing
   to sacrifice the poor on the altar of expediency.
And when it comes to the crunch
   Jesus cannot—and will not—
      collaborate with such an iniquitous system.
      Regardless of the consequences.

He does not have a death wish.
   He has no desire to die a martyr's death.

But, if death is the price he has to pay
for fighting for life and liberty, he'll pay it.

Jesus is committed.
There will be no compromise.
No taking a backward step.
And no turning back.

We may not face the same temptations. But any of us who are committed to the practice of compassion will inevitably face similar temptations sooner or later. Jesus shows us how to cope with those temptations.

We shouldn't be too self-conscious about the practice of compassion. We need to learn to simply give up trying to prove ourselves. We don't need to put ourselves down or beat ourselves up about trying to improve ourselves. We just need to become more forgetful of ourselves, and more mindful of others.

We shouldn't try to popularise the practice of compassion. We need to learn to simply live out our commitment to love and justice in our communities. We don't need razzmatazz or gimmicks to promote the movement. We just need some dignity, and the beauty of love and justice embodied in our communities will encourage all men and women of goodwill to continue to do good works as well.

We shouldn't try to compromise the practice of compassion. We need to learn to simply fight for the marginalised and disadvantaged in our society, without fear or favour. We don't need rockets or guns to combat the system. We just need some integrity, and the regard for the marginalised and disadvantaged represented in our struggle will encourage all men and women of goodwill to continue to struggle for their rights as well.

This is exactly the way Jim Dowling, Ann Rampa and the rest of the crew in the local Catholic Worker community seek to live their lives. The Catholic Worker movement was started sixty-odd years ago, on 1 May 1933, when Dorothy Day, a young journalist, suffragette, ex-communist and new convert to Christ, put out the first edition of the *Catholic Worker* newspaper for the May Day rally. Jim and Ann embraced the anarchist philosophy of the Catholic Worker movement, and set out, they say, 'not just to *work* for a new society, but to *be* a new society':

> We set out not just to serve the poor, but to live with the poor, and indeed to try to become poor by turning our backs on the seductions of our materialist society, and striving for a life of voluntary poverty.
>
> We set out not to improve our capitalist society, but to live as a sharing society, holding all things in common, and working cooperatively, to meet our basic needs.
>
> We set out not just to appeal to governments to change the violence of our society, but to non-violently resist these structures to the point of arrest and imprisonment.

This may sound very pretentious, but Jim and Ann are anything but pretentious as people. 'In all of these areas', they say, 'we have failed often. Yet', they say, 'we are always aware that faithfulness is more important than success, so we continue in faith to struggle, experiment and challenge one another to be a community that reflects the life of Christ.' Jim and Ann don't make a big deal about it, they just get on with it: providing hospitality, demonstrating cooperation, and practising resistance.

'We have always had more than one "Christ room" in our house,' they say, which is set aside 'for people needing support'. And there are always people needing support staying at Jim and Ann's house. 'We have attempted to work co-operatively to meet our basic needs by producing vegetable oil soap and fresh wholemeal bread, and, at various times, growing vegies and fruit trees, and making fragrant candles, and greeting cards. These industries, operated from home, have provided the bulk of our income.'

In 1984, Jim and Ann, and a few of their friends, opened Justice Products, to encourage people to buy 'justly produced commodities', especially merchandise produced by small co-ops like theirs, and boycott the 'products of slave labour'. Perhaps their best-known practice, is what they have termed 'resistance'.

We have endeavoured to live lives of non-cooperation with the institutionalised violence of war, poverty, racism, sexism, and...abortion. Politically, we have been involved in many issues, including free speech, justice for aboriginal people, affordable housing and environmental concerns. The impact of our resistance is often the hardest to gauge of all the things we do. Our message is often conveniently, if not deliberately, misunderstood.

Ain't that the truth! Because of their consistent pro-life stand, Jim and Ann have been constantly vilified by both the right and the left. In 1983 they decided to carry a banner reading "Defend Life: Stop Abortion and Nuclear Weapons", in a Right to Life rally, and then in a peace rally.

At the Right to Life Rally, when they tried to give out some leaflets, one man cried out, 'Don't take their leaflets, they're communists!' At the Peace Rally, people tried to hide their banner, and tear up leaflets, and when a friend took to the stage to defend their right of free speech, the microphone was wrested from his grasp by a woman who shouted, 'Typical Catholics! They just want to stop people f— ing!'[38]

I know Jim and Ann find this constant vilification difficult to cope with at times. I remember one time, especially, when Ann was spat on in the street, that hurt them deeply. But Jim and Ann have a poster on their wall, which they often reprint, which explains their perseverance in the face of opposition. It says:

> *When they come for the innocent,*
> *without crossing over your body,*
> *cursed be your religion!*

Intervention and frustration— and the Way of Christ

I am a bit of an activist myself. Over the years, I've come to know activists all over the world: people who are seriously engaged in a genuine struggle to advocate love and justice in their communities.

Most of the activists I know often feel a great sense of frustration: the frustration of aspiring to so much, yet accomplishing so little; of trying to get it together with others, but having to go it alone; of watching important programmes you have worked for long and hard, interrupted, disrupted and destroyed.

Even at the best of times, we all find these frustrations difficult to cope with. At the worst of times, they can be totally debilitating. It would appear that very few of us are coping very well. Many of us are so overwhelmed by the frustration of trying to translate our vision for a better world into tangible terms, that we have already all but given up the hope of ever making the dream come true.

Very few of us have learnt to live at peace with ourselves. The frustration without reverberates with the frustration within. The anxiety sets up an unhealthy vibration in our soul. And the un-ease eventually becomes dis-ease, which seriously affects our equilibrium.

Very few of us have learnt to live in companionship with others. We are either too independent, and alienate ourselves from the power to cope that a team can provide; or we are too co-dependent, and grow angry with the relationships that do not provide the power to cope that we had hoped for.

Very few of us have learnt to turn interruptions into opportunities. We insist on ideal conditions in which to live out our ideals. And when reality constantly interrupts our plans, and constantly wrecks our opportunities, we become more and more frustrated. We become uptight, so much so that we eventually explode. This is a great tragedy, because through these violent outbursts, those of us who are called to be agents of love and justice, can actually become agents of outrage and injury, and do more harm than good.

We need to learn to deal with these frustrations the way Jesus did. We need to imagine how Jesus dealt with them, and live through his experience, so that we can learn to deal with them as he did. Picture the situation as it was for Jesus, as he came face to face with these frustrations himself. 'Come,' says Jesus, 'I'll take you there.'

Jesus has just discovered his mission in life..

He has decided not only to be involved;
but also to take a lead in the movement.

He is determined to lead by personal example,
by embodying the ideals of the movement.

He is determined to be loving, and to be just,
and to give himself freely in service of others.
'The Spirit of God has gripped me,' he says,
'and has singled me out for a special task:
To share good news with the poor,
to free the prisoners,
to help the handicapped,
and to break the shackles of the oppressed.'
'I must let the people know
that the day of God's grace is upon us!'

For Jesus, this is not rhetoric; this is reality –
the reality he eats and drinks,
the reality he works for every day.

Every day
he makes time and space for the Spirit of God,
and he opens his soul to the Spirit of God;
his gut is ignited by the passion of God,
his bowels on fire with the compassion of God.

For him, empathy is not a superficial emotion,
but a deep gut-wrenching bowel-twisting sensation.
A visceral response to
the tears he sees, and the cries he hears,
And the suffering of others
that he feels, as if it were his very own.

He feels particularly anxious
about seeing desperately vulnerable people,

The Way of Christ

'sheep, without a shepherd,'
    with nobody there to protect them.

And he feels especially angry
    hearing about totally unscrupulous people,
'wolves, in sheep's clothing',
        taking advantage of that vulnerability.

'My grief is beyond healing,
    my heart is sickened within me,
because of the plight of the daughter of my people,
        from the length and the breadth of the land.

'For the wound
    of the daughter of my people,
        is my heart wounded.
I mourn, and dismay has taken hold of me.

'Can a woman forget
    a baby she has borne?
Can a mother refuse to care for
    the child at her breast?
Perhaps.' he says. 'Even these may forget.
But I will never forget you.

'Come to me,' he calls,
    beseeching the crowds,
the broken men, the battered women,
the abused children.

Christi-Anarchy

'Come to me, all you who are weary;
    crushed by carrying the burden of living.
Come to me, and I will offer you a place of rest,
    an oasis to restore your soul for the journey.
'Abide in me,' he tells them, 'and I'll abide with you.
    Together we'll be friends, you and I.
You can ask of me whatever you like,
    and I'll do it, because of my love for you.

'I want you to know my joy in you,
    and I want your joy in life to be full.'

And they do come, these lonely wanderers,
    these broken, battered and bruised.

A man dripping with leprosy,
    his body rank with running sores,
        his soul hungry for belonging.

Jesus reaches out to enfold him,
    to embrace him with love,
        to heal him with touch.

A woman, bleeding for twelve years;
    a dozen winters of rejection,
        her self-respect haemorrhaging.

Reaching out one last time,
    she finds Jesus and relief
        in the same beautiful moment.

'Go in peace,' he tells them,
   'your faith has made you whole.'

They come, and they keep coming,
   this troubled tribe of outcasts.
He tries to keep a lid on it, to keep it quiet.
   Cautions them to mute their enthusiasm;
      lest acts of kindness become circus acts.

But the winds blow,
   and the stories grow
      and the crowds gather.

The all-consuming masses, pushing and shoving,
   jostling like moths battering a single light.

They want this and they want that;
   they want to see a miracle,
      and they want to see more.

Jesus, at the centre of the chaos,
   is giving all he has to give,
      and still it is not enough.

He often feels he is on a hiding to nothing.

He wants to help people,
   but the more he does,
      the more they want him to do.

It is never ending.

But when he tells his disciples about it,
and they try to help him,
they just make matters worse.
When some parents bring their children
to him, to ask him to bless them,
the disciples push them away,
to prevent them from pestering him.

Jesus is incensed, and says,
'Hey. Let the little children come to me.'

He takes the eager children,
lifts them on to his lap, gives them a hug,
and blesses each of them, one by one.

Then he turns to his disciples,
and says, 'What are you doing?
This is what my work is all about!

The worst disease in the world is not leprosy –
it's being unacknowledged, being unwanted!'

But they take their toll,
these ravenous throngs.

Frustration clouds his compassion.

How to be pressed and yet patient;
how to be tired and yet care?

To dwell in the whirlwind,
in the midst of confusion and conflict,

without losing his vision,
Jesus knows he needs a quiet centre.

And he finds that still place,
where he can be at peace with himself
in the eye of the cyclone,
face to face with God.

Jesus nurtures the hideout in the canyon of his heart,
harbouring in it, and lingering in its shelter.

It is a cave in the midst of the commotion,
a quiet retreat in the midst of the action.

Here he enters and listens;
and hears the still small Voice once again.
'You are my Beloved.
In you I am well pleased.'

Fragrant, unconditional, limitless love,
running down, like thick olive oil,
into the recesses of his wounded soul.

Refreshing, renewing, reforming, redeeming grace.

Filling the void with the joy
of being loved, and being able to love.
A balm for frustration,
healing the deep hurt.
A wellspring of passion,
bubbling with compassion.

113

In it Jesus finds his strength, his stamina,
 for the endless rounds
 of giving and forgiving.
He learns the craft of caring,
 the hard task of loving
 friend and foe regardless.

Jesus realises that it is important
 for him to learn to care, himself, on his own,
 regardless of whether anyone else does or not.

But he also recognises that caring, is essentially
 a communal, rather than individual, activity,
 and that, even he, simply can not do it alone.

So he invites others to join him on the job,
 reviving the lost art of community care.

He is painfully aware
 of his friends' strengths and weaknesses,
 their gifts, and their frailties.

He knows
 he can't pin his hopes on them,
because, sooner or later, all of them,
 will, one way or another, let him down.

But he also knows
 that they can be good company,
and, in their own inept, but well-intended way,
 will be a great vanguard of love and justice.

In sharing their company, Jesus feels stronger.
They reflect and reaffirm his personal struggle.
In watching their faltering, clumsy, stumbling,
*   often very funny little attempts,*
*   to advance their great cause,*
*   Jesus gets a lot of encouragement,*
*   just to keep on going himself.*

'Together', he tells them, wryly,
*   we can change the world'.*

Change, he knows, is not so much in a strategy,
*   as it is in the ability of people, like them,*
to convert every interruption
*   into an opportunity to care,*
*   as constructively and productively as possible.*

Thus the movement
*   deepens and widens;*
the faltering ripple of hope
*   begins to extend outwards.*

Jesus shows us how to cope with frustrations.

We need to learn to live at peace with ourselves. We need to find a still point in our turning world, a quiet centre in the noisy vortex of our activities, where we can experience God's acceptance and affirmation, so that we can accept ourselves, affirm others, and act with equanimity.

We need to learn to live in companionship with others. We need to find a network of relationships, a community of family and friends in the midst of the multitudes, where we can be at home, open our hearts, let down our hair, put our feet up, and be ourselves with one another. In so doing, we can draw on the strength of the group, not to give up on our quest, but to keep on going, regardless of the consequences.

We need to learn to turn our interruptions into opportunities. We need to find a way of developing the art of embracing each difficult problem that we come across, every difficult person that we meet, and every frustration that we encounter, as a wonderful opportunity to express the spirit of compassion, the power of love and the possibility of justice.

This is exactly the way that Charles and Rita Ringma, and the people in Jubilee Fellowship, seek to live their lives. Jubilee Fellowship is an intentional community based in Brisbane, that Charles and Rita started some ten to fifteen years ago. It provides a support network for people who have come out of very dysfunctional situations, and who need to get into a much more healthy, hospitable, non-judgmental, supportive environment.

Like most of the communities I know that have intentionally taken in people who are distressed and disturbed, Jubilee Fellowship now has in its midst a microcosm of all the major difficulties that you can find in the world at large. Charles and Rita say, 'We need to learn to face our frustrations. These need not drive us to despair, but can bring us to find a new centre.'

This new centre 'can begin to be found when we meet with God. God does not necessarily relieve us of our burdens... [but] God embraces us' with our burdens, 'so that our burdens become light. It is from this centre... [this] place of fellowship [with the] God of all grace [that we can begin] to build families that are open, and friendships that are marked by reciprocity.'

However, Charles and Rita say, 'we can expect too much from others ... From those we love much, we often expect much, and from those we serve well, we frequently expect progress ... But our expectations may be unrealistic. Families can become ghettoes of unfulfilled expectations, and [friends] can be hurt when they expect too much from each other in the form of encouragement.'

'We need to realise that one of the greatest gifts we can give to others is the gift of freedom, where we allow the other person to take responsibility for their own responses ... We often think', they continue, 'that service is doing things *for* others. That sometimes needs to be. But service takes on its true character when we do things *with* others. This is never an easy road to travel. It is the slow road requiring much patience. It takes the pace *of* the other.' To be sure, there will be difficulties along the way, and 'difficulties often frustrate us: just one more thing on our plate that we don't have time for. We prefer to sidestep them. But it is difficulty that has inspired the human race to great creativity!'

In Jubilee Fellowship, people seek to cope with difficulty creatively through prayer, small supportive groups, and the development of their capacity to convert interruptions into opportunities.

There is an emphasis on prayer: a recognition that through prayer, through being in touch with faith in God, the community can derive the faithfulness that it needs to cope with the frustration, and still practice the compassion required to facilitate growth.

There is an emphasis on companionship, that is nurtured in the larger community organisation, through smaller support groups. These home-based groups provide a source of extended family-like support to help people in their struggle to generate healthy, functioning lifestyles.

There is an emphasis on the process of converting interruptions into opportunities. Regardless of how often their meetings are interrupted, plans are disrupted, and programmes are destroyed, the people never seem to give up. They simply help one another pick up the pieces, and put their lives back together again—and again.

Rather than allowing their frustrations to destroy their compassion, the activists in Jubilee Fellowship deal with them very creatively, continuing to advocate love and justice in the midst of the chaos that characterises so many of our communities these days.

'There is never an ideal time' to live out our ideals, say Charles and Rita. 'We have to seize the day. Grasp the opportunity. Make the most of good times and bad times. We must do what should be done, even when things are inconvenient: care for psychiatric patients, rehabilitation for drug addicts, and justice for minority groups. There is so much to do!'[39]

Salvation and suffering—and the Way of Christ

Quite a few of my friends are rebels, radicals and revolutionaries. Many have taken a stand in their communities that has turned their lives upside down and inside out. Many have started movements for personal growth and social change that have transformed significant sectors of their society.

Few, if any, have survived without scars. Some have been thrown out of their homes, ostracised by the very communities whose cause they advocated. Some have been thrown into prison cells and hospital wards, where they have been threatened with physical and psychological torture in an attempt to get them to renounce their commitment to profound political and economic transformation in society.

All revolution involves suffering. Violent revolutionaries may give as good as they get. Non-violent revolutionaries may do good for the evil done to them. But both violent and non-violent revolutionaries are wounded in a revolution.

All rebels, radicals, and revolutionaries bear their scars. The only ones who bear no scars are those who believe there is nothing worth fighting for. Every one of us who believes there is something worth fighting for, whether or not we are called rebels, radicals, and revolutionaries, will inevitably be scarred for life. We can be sure that in the course of the struggle to bring about love and justice, we will suffer.

We need to learn to deal with suffering the way Jesus did. We need to imagine how Jesus dealt with it, and live through his experience, so that we can learn to deal with it as he did. Picture the situation as it was for Jesus, as he came face to face with suffering himself. 'Come,' says Jesus. 'I'll take you there.'

The garden is very beautiful.

And Jesus has come to partake
*   of the beauty,*
*   of the quiet grass,*
*   and the strong, but gentle olive trees.*

He has come to pray
*   amidst the greenery and serenity*
*   of the garden of Gethsemane,*
*   enhanced enchantingly in the moonlight.*

It is a time of portent,
*   a night of decision, a moment for choosing.*

This drama of freedom
    that he's been directing,
is entering its denouement,
    its final vital phase.

He knows
    what he chooses to do now will be crucial.

Fulfilment and catastrophe
    lie waiting in the wings.

He could either lead the movement to triumph,
    or ruin everything he's been trying to accomplish.

Destiny is heavy in the air
    as he ponders his choices.

The hopes of a nation
    depend on how he will respond.
Yet the options he is confronted with are so painful.

So he has come
    to this place of solitude
        to contemplate his next move in peace.

Here and now, in the night air,
    his own words come back to haunt him.

He had said,
    'Compassion must prevail!
        Love and Justice above all!

'Over above and,
  if necessary, over and against,
all other political and economic considerations!'

And they had applauded his words to start with,
  congratulated him
    for his altruism and enthusiasm.

But when his ideals began to clash with their reality,
  rattling their cages, and stepping on their toes,
he had seen the faces turn away,
  with dark looks, and even darker hearts,
    and the murmuring had begun.

Each faction has its own complaint.
  Often quite different from that of another.
Yet each of the factions agrees
  that the movement advocated by Jesus,
    is at odds with their own vested interests.

'We might have been with you', they say,
  'if only you could have left well alone'.

The Consul, the King, and the Sanhedrin,
  all contest the plausibility
    of compassion as policy.
To say 'the rich should share their wealth with the poor'
  is 'tantamount to revolution!'
To ask 'everybody to love everybody, even their enemies',
  'amounts to an act of treason!'

On the one hand
   the Sadducees have their doubts about him;
because they believe in the status quo, and
   he threatens to overthrow the status quo.
'He'd make our slaves masters and our masters slaves!'

On the other hand,
   the Zealots have their doubts about him;
because he wants to overthrow the status quo
   non-violently,
and they believe that nothing less than
   violent change can overthrow the status quo.
'The only bit of ground the meek will inherit is a grave!'

As for the Pharisees, they believe that all this talk
   about compassion has gone too far.
'Charity is needed all right;
   but it should start at home,
      and it should stay at home.
It is unpatriotic for a Jew to suggest
   that charity should include the Samaritans!'

As for the Essenes, they have never heard of,
   let alone seen, a 'good' Samaritan.
'The only good Samaritan is a dead Samaritan.
   And any Jew who says otherwise
      is a bloody traitor to his own race!'

Even if they agree on nothing else at all,
the consul, the king, and the Sanhedrin,
   the Sadducees and the Zealots,

the Pharisees and Essenes, all agree
that Jesus,
and his message about love and justice,
is 'nothing but a pain in the bum of the body politic'.

Jesus knows this,
and is distressed by the growing opposition
from all quarters of society..

Alone in the garden,
he feels the pressure of advocating
an increasingly unpalatable
and unpopular cause;
he bears the pain of misunderstanding,
and the loneliness of isolation
that comes with rejection .

But he feels he cannot relent.
There is no scope, nor reason, for apology.

'God is compassionate,'
he cries from the depths of his beleaguered soul.
'We must be as compassionate as God is.'

He mocks the empty posturing of the orthodox Jews
And points to a heretical Samaritan
as a model of compassion.

He denounces empty rhetoric
and demands profound transformation
of the entire political economy.

He calls for a revolution
　　of love and justice
in which the roles
　　of the powerful
　　　　and the powerless
　　are turned completely upside down:
'The first will be last,
　　and the last will be first.'
'And the least among you
　　will be the greatest of all.'

He begs for immediate action
　　right here and right now.
'If not here, where? If not now, when?
　　Today is the day of salvation.'

He does not hesitate,
　　waiting for someone else to act;
　　he heeds his own advice and acts, decisively, himself.

He takes direct action against the Temple,
　　the financial clearing house of the kingdom,
　　　　the symbol of corruption and exploitation.

'This temple was meant to be a place of prayer!'
　　he screams,
　　　　as he scuttles the tables of the money changers.
　　'But you,
　　　　you have made it into a den of robbers!'

Still, Jesus isn't satisfied with challenging
the established structures of the current regime.

He wants to 'pour the new wine'
of his alternative movement,
into the 'new wineskins'
of intentional communities.

So he creates a network of anarchistic communities
in which his ideals can be realised, bit by bit.

To start with he teaches them
two startlingly new political and economic ideas:
'servant leadership' and 'common purse.'

The one,
a radical way of working things out with each other
by forgoing self-important protocol,
and facilitating group-decisions..

The other,
a radical way of sharing things with each other
by giving as much as is wanted,
and taking as much as is needed.

Jesus hopes these ideas
will be the seeds of inspiration
that will grow and
change the whole of society, from the ground up.

So he sends his disciples
out into the surrounding villages,
to sow these amazing seeds of transformation,
and to water them, and nurture them.

As the harvest
of political and economic change begins to ripen
it inevitably starts to threaten the status quo.

And Jesus soon finds
that he is officially designated
'a threat to society', 'a matter of state security'.

Jesus knows only too well what that means.

It isn't a surprise. He's been expecting it.
But it is still a shock when it happens.

He shudders as he thinks about it.
The chill shadows of consequence
fall across his troubled heart.

Jesus knows
that any 'threat to society'
will be eliminated
with swift and lethal efficiency.

So as a 'matter of state security'
it is only a matter of time
before the consul, the king and the Sanhedrin
get together, probably with the help

of the Sadducees and of the Pharisees,
to plot his arrest and execution.

The Essenes, no doubt, will stay out of it.
As, indeed, they stay out of everything.

The Zealots, his only hope of support,
will probably stay out of it as well.

Not because the Zealots are disgusted
with everyone and everything like the Essenes.

But because they are disappointed with him
and his persistent refusal to take up arms
in the service of the revolution.

So it is just a matter of time,
before the soldiers will be sent for him.

And nobody will stand beside him;
no one will stand in their way.

The garden is very beautiful,
especially in the evening.
But, as Jesus kneels in prayer,
it is not the beauty of the garden
that he beholds.

It is as if his dream of the world,
as a cup overflowing with life,
has become a nightmare.

Christi-Anarchy

So when he takes the cup into his hands,
   and he puts it to his lips,
the cup that is still overflowing
      with life for others
         has only death in it for him.

Others might drink deeply of its draughts,
      of laughter and smiles.
But not Jesus; to him it tastes, bitterly,
      of screams and tears .

Jesus has known all along that,
      sooner or later, it would come to this.

But now that the time has come for him
      to drink of the cup of suffering,
         he flinches, instinctively.

He is no masochist.
      Suffering holds no romance for him.
He doesn't relish the prospect of pain
      any more than any other man or woman.

Soon the soldiers will come for him
      With their warrant and their weapons.
They will bind him
      and take him away with them.
They will beat him,
      strip him naked in public.
         Just to humiliate him.

Then they will beat him some more.
  Scourge him with whips.
    Just for the hell of it.
And mock him in his moment of torment.

Then they will drag him to Golgotha,
  the dreaded Hill of the Skull.
Where they will make an example of him,
  by crucifying him on a cross.

It will not be a quick painless execution,
  but a slow painful death.
He will be used by the state
  as an object lesson in agony,
to discourage even the bravest soul
  from following in his footsteps.

So he prays, he cries, he pleads:
  'If it is possible,
    let this cup pass from me.'

But, deep in his heart, he knows.
Knows that suffering is used to discourage dissent,
  freedom of assembly,
    and freedom of action.
Knows that if he doesn't have the courage to suffer,
  for him,
    there can be no freedom.
Knows that the willingness to endure suffering
  always has been,

and always will be,
the essence of freedom.

And he knows, that the only way he can be free,
to be true to his vision of love and justice, is to suffer!

Has he not said so himself?
When he taught the multitudes
about salvation, grace and suffering?

Salvation, he had said,
is the redemptive experience
of the wonderful goodness of God.

And, on many occasions, he had said, that
people can discover salvation for themselves,
if they extend the same grace to one another,
as God, in his goodness, extends towards them.

If they exorcise the demonic impulse
to do evil for good;
renounce the human reaction
to do evil for evil, and good for good;
and embrace the divine response,
to do good for evil.

And he had said—had he really said it?—
that to do good for evil,
depends on the willingness to suffer evil,
without wanting to do any evil in return.

Salvation is eminently—immanently—possible.
But there is no salvation without grace,
and no grace without suffering.

And now, for Jesus, the time has come
to practise what he has preached!

Jesus remembers
the power that voluntary suffering
can have in bringing about great change.

Dying for a cause doesn't make it right.
But a manifesto written in the blood of its devotees
is not lightly discounted, nor easily disregarded.
A movement which has proved worth dying for
may lay claim to be considered worth living for.

If his martyrdom lights a beacon for compassion
then his crucifixion will not be in vain.
Jesus recognises
that his own voluntary suffering
could have unique power, peculiar to him.

People know him,
know his convictions, his character, his innocence.
His demise might light an inextinguishable fire
that scorches the earth of its unrighteousness.

His agony
might break people's hearts,

and in the process
break down their barriers
of apathy, insensitivity and hypocrisy.

His anguish
might bring the sound of crying
to the ears of those
who, otherwise, would not hear,
and bring insight, through tears,
to the eyes of those
who, otherwise, would not see.

His pain
might invoke sympathy
from the heart of humanity.

His pathos
might convert the soul
of the whole of his world.

His death
need not be the end;
but might be a birth,
the beginning of a new age!

So, finally, Jesus prays,
'Not my will, but yours be done'.

He rises from the place
where he has been praying.

He bears no weapon,
save his agenda for love and justice.

And when the soldiers come
to take him away,
Jesus steps forward,
with arms outstretched,
in welcome,
to embrace the very men,
who will nail his hands and his feet to the cross.

Jesus shows us how to approach suffering.

We need to realise that suffering, rather than being an optional extra for masochistic fanatics, is the inevitable fate of all activists, whether they are masochists or not. Without suffering, there may be much dialogue, there may be many debates, but little will be done in terms of converting our world to any significant degree. Salvation is only possible through suffering.

None of us likes suffering. But if we allow our fear of suffering to prevent us from promoting love and justice, then our fear becomes cowardice. And the consequences of cowardice for our world are catastrophic. We are immobilised, unable to do the good that we need to do, due to our fear of evil. Then evil triumphs, as it always does, when we don't do the good we know we ought to do.

We cannot save the world if we are cowards; to save the world we will need to be heroes. But we need to remember that heroes are generally not fearless people; rather they are fearful, but act in spite of their fear. The opposite of cowardice is not the absence of fear, but courage in the face of fear.

All healthy human beings fear suffering. Fear of suffering, in fact, is essential to our survival as healthy human beings. But, like

Christ, we must be prepared to suffer voluntarily, personally, wherever and whenever necessary, to practice compassion in circumstances hostile to love and justice.

We must be willing to suffer gladly for the sake of others, so that they can know the real meaning of love, and so they can say of us, as they said of Christ, 'this is love, not that we loved him but he loved us, and laid down his life for us' (1 John 3:16). And we must be willing to suffer the loss of all things, giving everything and forgiving everything, so that we can ensure that people experience the encouragement of our common quest with them for justice. As Christ said, 'those who do justice will shine like the sun' (Matthew 13:43).

This is exactly the way that Edmund Cocksedge, and some of the other folk at the House of Freedom discipleship community, have sought to live their lives. Very few of them would regard themselves as rebels, radicals, or revolutionaries, though many people in our neighbourhood would regard them as such, referring to them affectionately as 'a bunch of ratbags.' However, the people in the House of Freedom are the kind who believe that love and justice are causes worth fighting for, and some of them, like Edmund Cocksedge, have actually fought for these causes – non-violently of course – for the whole of their lives.

Edmund was born in 1915, in England, just after the outbreak of World War I. He was brought up in the cathedral city of Canterbury, in a devout nonconformist Congregational family. While still a young man, Edmund moved to London, to study and to work as an optician. There he got involved with the Bloomsbury Baptist Church, and through them, with helping young people who were 'doing it tough' on the council estates. He also got involved with the Tramp Preachers, who preached radical identification with the poor, and the Peace Pledge Union, who practised revolutionary non-violent intervention in times of conflict in the hope of securing peace.

At the age of twenty-one, as war was looming large with Germany, Edmund decided to go to Germany to make contact with the Bruderhof, a community of passionate anti-Nazi pacifists, who were being persecuted by the Nazis for their implacable opposition to militarism. It was hard for the young Edmund to decide to go to Germany at that time, because some of his closest family and friends were quite bitter about it, and 'argued against the concepts I expressed.'

It was even harder for the young Edmund when he got to Germany, because the Bruderhof were suffering for their stand against the state; they were very poor, and under constant surveillance by the Gestapo, who conducted random raids of the community, to command compliance, and to confiscate further property if that compliance was not forthcoming.

Edmund returned to England an older and wiser man, committed more than ever to simplicity, solidarity, community and nonviolence. He established connections with the anarchists in Spain, supporting their struggle against fascism, but 'experienced great tension' criticising the atrocities committed by both sides in the Spanish Civil War. He also linked up with the non-violent activists or *satyagrahis* in India, supporting their struggle against the imperialism of his own country, and risking being branded a traitor for his advocacy of the Indian Independence Movement. Meanwhile, against the background of the build-up for war against Germany, Edmund and his friends in the Peace Pledge Union, decided to go on a Peace Trek round England encouraging conscientious objection.

By and large the Peace Trek was peaceful. But at one demonstration against military recruitment at a big army exhibition, Edmund and his friends found themselves surrounded by a furious crowd, which Edmund describes, with his typical English understatement, as 'making angry verbal attacks on us'.

After the Peace Trek Edmund married his great friend and fellow peace activist, Amy, and they joined the Fellowship of Reconciliation, a well-known international peace network, and began the Elmsett Community, a community base for peace activists. Then World War II broke out.

During the war Edmund and Amy registered as conscientious objectors, and volunteered to do vital agricultural work for the country. At the same time they got involved with refugees from the Bruderhof in Germany, who were seeking asylum in England. It turned out that as pacifists, the Bruderhof were not welcome in Germany, but as Germans, they were not welcome in England. So they had to reconsider relocation elsewhere. They eventually decided on Paraguay, and Edmund and Amy offered to go with them, to help them resettle there.

So they and their young family travelled with some sixty refugees across the perilous Atlantic, 'in silence, and without any kind of lights showing', so as to avoid the attention of enemy U-Boats, in the middle of the war, seeking safety in South America. When they got there they joined another couple of hundred refugees, who in turn sponsored another hundred, and together they built a series of very simple, but very peaceful, self-sustaining community farms in a place called Primavera.

Life was hard. The climate was hot—very hot indeed for the German pacifists and their English friends. And the work was painstaking, back-breaking physical labour. But in spite of the sicknesses, which laid many of the settlers low, and actually took the lives of some of their leaders, Edmund has great memories of his twenty years in Primavera. However, after Amy gave birth to their ninth child, she developed heart trouble, and Edmund felt they should go back to England for the sake of her health. So the family returned to England.

Tragically, on their return, Amy was killed in a car crash, leaving Edmund disconsolate and directionless. However, in 1972, just when the House of Freedom was starting up in Brisbane, Edmund was invited over by one of his daughters, who had migrated to Australia. When he met up with people from the House, Edmund was overjoyed, because like him, they were committed to a simple lifestyle, servant leadership, common purse, and direct non-violent action.

For Edmund, it was to prove a whole new beginning. He threw himself into the life and work of the House of Freedom. Even at the age of sixty, Edmund often left the twenty- and thirty-year-olds way behind, particularly when it came to 'witnessing for peace and justice' through direct non-violent action. Edmund was arrested at the Anglican Cathedral for protesting the complicity of the church with the state over the Vietnam War. And I can remember standing shoulder to shoulder with an eighty-year-old Edmund Cocksedge outside the Brisbane City Hall, protesting against the Gulf War.

Edmund is the kind of hero that we need to be: not famous, but faithful; not fearless—'in our hearts', he says, 'we were always fearful'—but courageous nevertheless.[40]

Perseverance and despair—
and the Way of Christ

Recently a leading Australian evangelical Aboriginal human rights advocate I knew, felt so discouraged by the plight of his people that he hanged himself. None of us who campaign for human rights, in a context of callous disregard for the rights of others, will be able to avoid experiencing such moments of total and utter despair ourselves. From time to time we all have cause to cry, like Christ: 'My God, My God, why have you forsaken me?'

We need to learn to deal with this despair the way Jesus did. We need to imagine how Jesus dealt with it, and live through his experience, so that we can learn to deal with despair, the way Jesus did. Picture the situation, as it was for Jesus, as he came face to face with despair himself. 'Come,' says Jesus. 'I'll take you there.'

After everything is said and done;
the Gospel proclaimed,
the Spirit displayed,
the possibilities presented,
the people empowered;
Jesus is confronted with what everyone
who has ever sought to change the world
is left with in the end:
total and utter despair.

Mind-numbing,
strength-sapping,
soul-destroying despair.

It is a galaxy of nothingness and nobodyness
which lurks in the heart's dark interior.

It is a gaping hole at the centre of the heart,
into which meaning and energy tumble.

It is a quagmire at the bottom of the heart,
where the dreams life bears lie stillborn.

Jesus' despair begins
with the realisation that,
among the multitudes who follow him,
there is only a handful he can trust.

When he comes to Jerusalem
at the Passover Feast
many believe in him
when they see the signs he does.

But he does not trust himself to them
because he knows the people well,
and he knows how seldom they
take such belief very seriously.

His despair grows when the crowds
that gather behind him in Galilee,
rallying round the ringing cry for revolution,
simply give up the struggle,
turn their back on him, and go back home,
when it comes time to pay their dues.

His despair grows when the crowds
that gather before him in Jerusalem,
singing his praises, applauding his miracles,
quickly sidestep his agenda,

deflect his challenge, dismiss his criticism,
and go about their business as usual.

'O Jerusalem, Jerusalem,' *he cries,*
'*killing the prophets, and stoning the seers.*
How often
would I have gathered your children together
as a hen gathers her brood under her wings,
but you would not.'

When he draws near to the city,
he weeps over it, saying:
"*Would that even today*
you knew the things that make for peace.'
But they could not—would not—even try to understand,
the things he said that make for peace.

His despair grows even greater when it becomes obvious
that one of his friends is going to betray him,
and all of his other friends are going to run away,
at the very time when he needs them most.

Not even one of his closest companions seems to be
able to stand beside him in his hour of need.

He remembers asking his disciples, one by one,
'*Couldn't you keep watch with me for one hour?'*

But there is no answer.
Only a long embarrassed silence.

He is abandoned. He is alone.
  And he knows it.

All that is left for him is that, abandoned and alone,
  he will be faithful in the crucible of torment.

That he, at least,
  will die with dignity for what he believes in.
That he, at least,
  will lay down his life for the issues at stake.
That he, at least,
  will be a martyr for the sake of love and justice.

But Jesus' despair,
  which has grown daily throughout his ministry,
grows even greater, when his moment of truth comes;

A tidal wave
  of terrible sorrow utterly overwhelms him,
engulfing him in an anguish,
    from which there is no escape.

It mocks him
  with his dream of what might have been,
while crushing him
  with the reality of what is happening.

His final act of heroic resolve
  is totally misconstrued
by the throng standing around the foot of the cross.

They don't see him as a courageous radical,
    dying for the people in the struggle for freedom.

To them, 'He's a crook! A criminal!'

They don't speak of him as an enlightened soul,
    sacrificing his life for the sake of his friends.

To them, 'He's a fool! An idiot!'

They don't weep for him;
    they laugh at him;
chortling among themselves about his impotence.

'He could save others,' they scoff,
    'but cannot save himself!'

Now Jesus' despair is monstrous.

Here on his lonely wooden cross,
    his sense of the futility of it all
        grabs him by the throat
and begins to slowly throttle him.

Has it come to this? He wonders.
All that he has sought to say and do—
    has it all merely come to this?
        To this—
        this travesty of compassion?

Has he, by his death, only managed
   to succeed in convincing everyone
   that everything that he has lived for—is false?

Is his mission, in the end,
   a complete mockery of love and of justice?

'Eli. Eli, lama sabachthani—' he cries.
   'My God. My God, why have you forsaken me?'

The silence is deafening.
   The heavens empty of comfort.

His humiliation is complete;
   his body wracked with pain;
     his soul broken with disappointment.

And yet, in spite of his loss,
   Jesus gambles on grace for one more time.

In one final act of trust
   he flings himself into 'the everlasting arms'.

Not seeing, nor hearing, scarcely breathing,
   Jesus casts his spirit into the mystery of God.

'Father,' he says, expiring,
   'into your safe keeping I commit my spirit'.

Any of us who have experienced despair know how soul-destroying it can be. But somehow Jesus was able to survive the experience. Indeed, he was not only able to survive it, but also able to emerge from it with the resolute courage of his convictions stronger than ever before.

If we are going to survive the experience of despair with this same resolute courage, then we need to deal with it as Jesus did.

I want us to note three points. The first is that: *Jesus accepted despair as a part of life, indeed, as a prerequisite for life!* For Jesus, despair was not only as much a part of life as hope, but it was also that part of life through which hope became meaningful for life. For Jesus, life could only be found by those who had lost it.

It is through an experience of profound despair, when all false hopes are so irrevocably destroyed, that we can experience, in our 'nothingness', the possibility of hope in God, plus 'nothing'.

Those of us who encounter despair need to remember this point: that hope is born in despair, with God.

The second point is that *Jesus continued to practise what he believed in even when it seemed in vain; indeed, his practice of love and justice was perfected in futility.* For Jesus, despair was the test of true virtue, which is practised without hope of reward. For Jesus, real giving involved giving without any hope of return, and real forgiving involved forgiving without any hope of revenge.

It is as we experience despair, and give up all hope of being able to change anyone or anything, that our practice of virtue becomes less a carefully planned strategy to gain a certain set of objectives and more an expression of solidarity with people whose limitations and contradictions we experience in our own lives.

Those of us who encounter despair need to remember that, with God, true virtue can mature through an experience of despair, because with God, through an experience of despair, we can become less manipulative and more compassionate.

The third point is that *Jesus entrusted himself and his cause to God in spite of the unsolved problems, the unanswered questions, the pain that wracked his body, and the despair that tortured his soul; indeed, in spite of the fact that God seemed so very far away, he put his trust in God to be there to care for him and vindicate his cause, by saying 'Father, into your safe keeping I commit my spirit'.* In doing so Jesus was able to flesh out his faith in God as he had never been able to before. In fact Jesus could give no greater testimonial to God than this: that at such a time of terrible doubt, he entrusted himself and his cause solely to God.

It is as we experience despair, when God seems more absent than present, when we struggle with unsolved problems and unanswered questions to the point of painful desperation, that we have our greatest opportunity to flesh out our faith in God. For our faith in God is most profoundly expressed when the temptation to denounce him is met with a resounding demonstration of trust in his capacity to care for us and vindicate our cause.

Those of us who encounter despair need to remember that our greatest opportunity to glorify God is when all hope is gone and, hoping against hope, we gather up the last vestiges of our anguish and struggle, and gamble all we hold dear—for ourselves and our society—on God, as C.S. Lewis puts it:

> when a human, no longer desiring, but still intending, to do [God's] will, looks round upon a universe from which every trace of Him seems to have vanished, and asks why he has been forsaken, and still obeys.[41]

It was Australia Day. Most of Australia was celebrating the birth of the nation, as usual, with ticker-tape parades in the city streets, and barbecues in backyards. But the birth of our modern society is predicated upon the death of an ancient civilisation. Surely this is more of a reason for sorrow than for celebration, particularly for the Aboriginal and Islander people, on the bones of whose ancestors our so-called civilisation has been built.

Indigenous people lived in Australia for some 40,000 years before the arrival of settlers from Europe. When the first migrants arrived, there were about 300,000 Aborigines and Islanders; but after a hundred years of systematic slaughter and resettlement, there were barely 50,000 Aborigines and Islanders left alive, and few of those who survived had any access to their sacred ancestral land.

So while Australia Day might be a party time for non-indigenous Australians, it is a time of grief, anger, and despair for indigenous Australians. On Australia Day, while the rest of Australia was kicking up its heels, Pastor Henry Collins, a local Murri leader, was taking his stand in Musgrave Park—once traditional Murri land—under a red, black and yellow Aboriginal flag, that he was flying at half-mast as a symbol of mourning for all disenfranchised indigenous Australians.

'The creation is groaning in travail', say Pastor George Rosendale and the Rainbow Spirit Elders. 'We know only too well the suffering of our people since the invasion of Australia. But the land also suffers. Our forefathers had laws about caring for the land. They knew the land is sacred and that people belong to the land.'

> The Europeans did not know the law of the land. They brought in many plants and animals from Europe and elsewhere which hurt and destroyed God's wonderful creation here in Australia. They brought in farming methods from Europe which also destroyed God's creation. We see them killing the land and the

plants and the animals with bulldozers, bushfires, erosion, and sometimes killing for no reason they do not even eat what they kill ... Our people were appointed caretakers by the Creator Spirit, but in many places we cannot carry out our responsibility any more. Others have taken over control without knowing the law of the land. We groan because the land suffers, and the land groans because we suffer.[42]

'The pain is like that of a parent losing a child.' the Rainbow Spirit Elders say. 'Many Aboriginal people do not realise that our suffering is a result of our losing our spiritual connection with the land. When Aboriginal people are taken from our spiritual homes we also lose our spiritual contact with the Creator Spirit.'

'Stealing our land is not like stealing a cow.' they say. 'Stealing our land means stealing our souls, stealing what is most precious to us, stealing our strength, our stories and our songs, our link with the Creator Spirit. Stealing our land means taking our lives. It is murder.'[43]

The Rainbow Spirit Elders then recount a long, painful, and yet incomplete list of atrocities that their people have had to endure:

- the imposition of European customs that were tantamount to enslavement;
- the designation of Aboriginal human beings as sub-human and racially inferior;
- the massacre of innocent Aboriginal groups by official government parties;
- the hunting down of Aboriginal people like wild animals;
- the poisoning of billabongs and waterholes to exterminate Aboriginal families;
- the sexual abuse of Aboriginal women by people associated with missions;

- the forceful removal of Aboriginal children from their families;
- the humiliation of Aboriginal people with shameful public punishment;
- the death of humiliated Aboriginal young people in police custody;
- the vilification of Aboriginal spirituality as barbaric and demonic;
- the desecration of Dreaming places and other sacred sites.[44]

'We see Christ,' they say, 'suffering in our people who have been separated from their land, who are paupers on the fringes of Australian society, and whose spirits continue to be crushed through the taunts of others. But Christ not only suffered, he also rose victorious over evil! For us the Rainbow Spirit, who has suffered in Christ, is now rising again to free our people!'

Even though we have been dispossessed of our lands, even though our life-giving spiritual tradition has been dismissed as idle fairy tales, even though our supportive extended family structure has been denigrated as primitive, even though our spirits have been crushed as we have internalised what others have said about us, we stand confident and bold and declare:

If God be for us, who can be against us!
Neither death,
*   nor life;*
Neither angels,
*   nor rulers;*
Neither things present,
*   nor things to come;*
Nor anything else,

in all of creation,
Will be able to separate us
from the love of God,
Revealed to us through
Jesus Christ our Lord![45]

Pastor Henry Collins concluded by calling all of us who were there on that Australia Day, to join him under the flag, in a time of prayer.

Father, Mother, God,
you gave us the Dreaming.
You have spoken to us through our beliefs.
And You made your love clear to us in Jesus.
We thank You for Your care.
You are our only hope.
Make us strong
as we face the problems of change.
We ask You to help the people of Australia
to listen to us and respect our culture.
Make the knowledge of You
grow strong in all people,
so that You can be at home in us
and we can make a home
for everyone in our land. Amen.

By entering into prayers such as this, we can move, like Christ—with Pastor Henry Collins, Pastor George Rosendale, and the Rainbow Spirit Elders—from total and utter despair, towards hope in the midst of despair; and in so doing, embrace the practice of virtue, in spite of our futility, and the importance of faith in God, for the sake of our otherwise God-forsaken cause.

The Spirit of Christ: the hope of humanity

But it's easier to say than to do. How can any of us expect to incarnate compassion—and embody love and justice, in our personal and corporate lives—in a world that is so obsessed with 'ethnic cleansing'? It is a question every activist, no matter how active, asks themselves late at night, after a long hard day, when they find themselves alone with their thoughts in bed.

It is a question my friend, Doctor Deenabandu, couldn't stop thinking about, day and night, till he stopped thinking altogether. Doctor Deenabandu had met Mahatma Gandhi while still a young man. He'd just got out of medical school, graduated as a doctor, and was raring to go. As a result of his meeting with Gandhi, Doctor Deenabandu decided to dedicate his life to the service of the 'outcastes' in his society.

It was an exciting time. The Independence Movement was on a roll. The New India they envisaged would be an India for all Indians, regardless of whether they were high caste, low caste, or had no caste at all. Mahatma Gandhi had renamed the God-forsaken outcastes of society *harijans*—sons and daughters of God. Congress Party had outlawed untouchability or disassociation from the *harijans*. So it was a great time to take up their cause.

Doctor Deenabandu threw himself into his work for the *harijans*, body and soul, day and night, for the next fifty years. However things did not work out as he had envisaged. At the end of those fifty years of work, Doctor Deenabandu was forced to conclude that they were no better off than when he had begun; in fact, he thought, they were probably worse off. They were not only poor; but actually poorer than before. The policy of affirmative action had backfired big time; and the level of prejudice in the general society against them had escalated alarmingly. Many of them so hated the honourable name, *harijan*, that Gandhi had given them, that they took the name *dalit* instead, to refer to their deprived and oppressed state.

One day the hopelessness of the situation, that he had worked the whole of his life to address, became too much for Doctor Deenabandu to bear any more, and he just switched himself off, like he'd turned off the light. From then on, Doctor Deenabandu, who had done everything he could for everyone, did absolutely nothing. He just sat in the corner of a room, staring vacantly into space, like a disused table lamp that had once taken pride of place at family meals round the dining table, but was now of no use at all to anyone.

I can only ever remember hearing him speak once. I'd gone to visit him, and tried as usual to engage him in conversation, to no avail. As I was sitting there with him in the silence, I began to wonder out loud, 'I wonder what Gandhiji would think about the situation now?'

Before I knew what was happening a terribly sad and bitter voice, which I had never heard before, spoke from the corner of the room, where Doctor Deenabandu was sitting, as still as a statue, and said: 'Where is Gandhiji now? He's just a statue in the city that the birds shit on!'

I turned immediately in Doctor Deenabandu's direction, scarcely able to believe that he had spoken and scarcely able to believe what he had said. Did he actually speak? Or was I imagining it? Did he actually say what I thought he said? Or was I projecting it?

As soon as I saw the look on his face, turned to look at me for the very first time—his eyes filled to overflowing with tears, that were streaming down his cheeks—I knew that he had indeed spoken, and what he had said had come from the depths of his soul.

For Doctor Deenabandu the truth was that he felt he'd gambled the whole of his life on *sarvodaya,* he service of the poor, the poorest of the poor—and he'd lost it, wasted it all. All the blood, sweat and tears of fifty years—*fifty years!*—had all gone down the gurgler; and on top of that, his mentor was dead, and there was no-one for him to turn to for the inspiration he needed to be able to carry on.

Doctor Deenabandu had fought the good fight. But without hope in the midst of the hopelessness, he had got to the stage where he couldn't fight any more. It just didn't make sense. So he simply gave up.

And unless we can find some hope for ourselves, in the midst of the hopelessness of trying to incarnate compassion and embody love and justice, in our personal and corporate lives, in a world obsessed with 'ethnic cleansing', then sooner or later—certainly a whole lot sooner than the dedicated Doctor Deenabandu—we will give up too.

When Christ was crucified, the hope of his disciples, that they actually may have been able to build a better world together, was totally shattered. In the hopelessness that ensued, all of them, particularly Peter, decided to give up the dream—which had become a nightmare—as a bad joke.

Picture the situation as it was for Peter, as he tried to put the pieces of his life together, after the dream was over and the reality of the situation came crashing down around him.[46]

Casting his mind back on it now,
    even years later down the track,
Peter could still taste the bitterness
    of the despair that he'd felt then.

Jesus was dead.
    And all their hopes were buried with him.

He didn't know who to believe,
  or what to believe in any more.

He didn't even know
  whether he wanted to live, or die.

Some of the others
  came to him with some wild stories
    about seeing Jesus alive.

But he had told them to wake up to themselves.
  The dream was over. It was time to face reality.

Jesus was dead and buried.
      End of story.

They could go on with their illusions if they wanted to.
  But he was going back,
    back to where he came from,
  back to the only reality
    that he still knew anything about.

He didn't know anything about faith any more.
  The only thing he knew anything about was fishing.

So he had decided,
  to go back home and
    take up fishing once again.

As soon as he got back to Galilee,
  he grabbed the family boat,

and went out fishing for the night,
with a few of his close friends.

Nothing like going fishing at night with some mates
to ease the pain and the disappointment of the day.

The darkness warm and welcoming,
the gentle lap of water calming to the nerves.

But, as it turned out,
it was a very frustrating night for fishing.

Everything went wrong. Nothing worked out right.

They tried all their favourite spots.
Down by the sand bank. Near the river entrance.
But they caught nothing. Absolutely nothing.

What a waste of time
it had been, being with Jesus;
All this talk about building a better world,
but it had been nothing but trouble,
and now here he was, a professional fisherman,
and he couldn't fish to save himself!

Then, he had heard it: the Voice!
Clearly across the water.

There was something about the timbre of it
that sent shudders up and down his spine.

The Way of Christ

He turned, and peered through the darkness,
but saw nothing more than the gathering dawn.

I must be jumpy, he had thought, letting the swell
bring the memory up from the heaving depths.

But there it was again:
the Voice!
That unmistakable still small Voice.

This time there was no possibility of denying it.
It brought back a thousand mixed emotions.

'Oh no!' He'd thought, gut wrenching. 'Not again!'

It couldn't be.
He's dead and buried.
Lying silent in a grave.

Against his better judgment,
Peter had found himself listening
for the sound of the Voice.

What was it saying? Something about the fish?.
About being able to catch
the fish on the other side of the boat?

It didn't make much sense to him,
but, then again,
he hadn't caught anything all night,

Christi-Anarchy

so he had thought
he had nothing to lose, if he gave it a go.

As soon as he did,
he felt the old familiar rush,
that he always got, when he got a big catch.

He saw the nets take the strain,
and heard fish begin to thrash,
as they hauled a large shoal to the surface.

Nets straining, fish thrashing, men laughing.
As big a catch as he'd ever got!

'My God!' Peter had sighed. 'He's back!'

In that moment
the veneer of his restraint
splintered to matchwood.

Unable to contain himself,
Peter had jumped for joy,
leapt out of the boat,
before it got to the shore,
splashed into the sea,
and run through the shallows
towards the figure he saw,
shimmering through the tears,
standing waiting on the beach.

156

When he had actually got to Jesus
    Peter stopped a few paces short –
        caught by conflicting emotions:
    on the one hand so excited,
        he wanted to embrace him,
    on the other hand, so scared,
        he wanted to run away.

But then he had looked at Jesus –
    gazed into those kindly eyes,
        moistened with poignant understanding;
    gaped at that gentle smile,
        spread from ear to ear with unfeigned joy;
    stared at the strong hands
        outstretched towards him, in welcome,
    and, before he knew it,
        Peter literally fell into Jesus' arms.

They had embraced,
    for what seemed an eternity
while the shouting crew dragged the boat to the beach.

Then Jesus invited Peter, and his friends,
    to share a hot breakfast that he'd cooked for them.

Over breakfast they began to talk.

After some banter,
    some gallows humour
    about crucifixions and resurrections,

Jesus gently - very gently - raised the subject
of their betrayal of him at the death.

Suddenly the conversation ground to a halt.
Each of the disciples intently studying
the flames that flickered
in the cooking fire
at the centre of their circle.

Then Jesus had turned to Peter, and said,
'What's done is done;
we all make mistakes.
I'm not one to bear resentments.
The last thing I want to do
is hold what you did
against any of you.'

'But there is one thing
I want to sort out
with you, if I can.
Both for your sake and mine.'

The flames flickered among the embers,
and the smoke hung in the morning air.

'It's a question I need to ask,
and which I'd like you
to answer, honestly. All right?'

They nodded, embarrassed,
in the early morning light.

'Well, all I want to know is—
   do you really love me?'

''Cause if you don't—
   if you don't really care for me,
      or the things I really care for,
   all this is a waste of time.'

'But if you do—
   if you really care for me,
      and the things I really care for,
   then I want to assure you
      no matter how often you fail me,
   I'll never ever fail you;
      I'll never leave you,
   or forsake you,
      or ever let you down;'

'I'm prepared to move
   heaven and earth to help
      you build a better world,
   bit by bit, out of the ruins
      of your broken dreams.'

'Now—tell me, I need to know,
   do you really love me?'.

Peter never forgot that moment.
   As time merged with eternity.
He always felt that
   it was the defining moment of his life.

He remembered, even now, how he'd said,
with the blood throbbing in his ears,
'Jesus, I know
you'd like me to love you,
like you love me—
unconditionally.

But I can't promise you that.
I've tried to do it, but I can't.

'What I can promise you is that
I'll do my best—
and maybe, with your help,
do better than my best—
to be your very closest friend,
to hang out with you,
to do the things that
you want to do ... together.

'And you never know,
along the way, maybe, together,
we can work something out.'

Suddenly there's a new warmth in the morning air.

Was it the fire that brought the warmth,
or did it come from something else?

Peter never knew.

But Peter had felt the warmth
when Jesus turned to him and said,

'Well, Peter, that sounds pretty good to me.
If you'd like to give it a go,
I'd like to give it a try.
Perhaps we could work on a project together?
Like nurturing our "flocks".

Peter had looked at Jesus and smiled.
'Sure!' he said laconically. 'Let's do it!'

And so the course of Peter's life was set
and the big fisherman was pushed out into the tide.

Creating alternative non-violent communities,
which reflected the relentless tenderness
of his friend, the 'once-dead-and-buried' Jesus,
became Peter's mission in life.

At the time, of course,
he had no way of knowing what would come of it.

But he remembered that great day in Jerusalem,
when he'd got everybody together again,
and the Spirit had come upon them, like a monsoon,
and, as demoralised as they all had been,
they had all been drenched with energy and enthusiasm.

They had been renewed, revived, and come alive again,
as if Jesus had been resurrected in them!

High on the scent of freedom,
bubbling with the joy of life and liberty,

they had begun to rebuild their world,
bit by bit,
out of the ruins of their broken dreams –
just as Jesus said they would.

Those early days were great days.

They all had met together.
Breaking bread in their homes
and eating together with glad and jubilant hearts.
They had everything in common.
Selling their possessions,
and giving support to anyone who asked for help.

So there wasn't a single person
with an unmet need among them.
And all the people spoke well of them.

It was as if their prayer for God's will
to be done on earth, as it is in heaven,
had actually come to pass.

Almost, but not quite.

There had been a storm cloud
that had darkened the horizon
and threatened the bliss of those sunny days;

And that was the perennial problem of all communities,
even alternative communities:
the problem of exclusivity.

The Way of Christ

Most of the members of the communities were,
like Jesus, traditional, religious Jews;
and for them, to open up their closed communities
to include others, non-traditional Jews,
let alone Gentiles, was unthinkable.

Peter remembered how it had taken
a public brawl with Paul,
and a painful debriefing with Jesus,
to convince him that their communities
needed to be inclusive of all people,
regardless of tradition, culture or religion.

Paul had told him:
'Sure, there's a difference
between Jews and Gentiles.
But those differences needn't be
a cause for division between them.

'Jesus' purpose was to create,
in himself and in everything he stood for,
one united humanity,
by destroying the dividing wall of hostility,
that had been built on the basis of
traditional, cultural and religious differences.'

But Peter still wasn't convinced,
until Jesus visited him in a vision,
and confronted him, face to face,
with the unacceptability of exclusivity:
labelling some people, 'clean'
and others 'unclean'.

Jesus, Peter remembered,
  had thundered at him, in no uncertain terms:.
'Don't you dare ever to relate to people as 'unclean''
  when God has declared them 'clean'!'

Then, and only then, had Peter conceded,
  and finally been forced to acknowledge
    that God does not show favouritism
    but accepts people from every nation,
      who revere him and do what is right.

And from then on,
  the communities that Peter had established,
  that were dedicated to God's dream for love and justice,
    being done on earth, as it is in heaven -
  were open to all people
    as 'chosen people'.

And over the years the big fisherman's heart
  was broken time and time again,
as he came to see the breath-taking beauty
  of people, who were once no people -
    rejected and neglected and ignored -
  become chosen people,
    accepted and respected and affirmed
    as the people of God.

Miroslav Volf is a Croatian. His family, along with hundreds of thousands of others in the former Yugoslavia—Croatia, Serbia and Bosnia—have been torn apart by civil war, and by what has come to be known as 'ethnic cleansing.'

Volf says that the problem of ethnic cleansing is not specific to the Balkans. Now that modern transportation and telecommunications have turned the whole world into a single global multicultural economy, he says that it is a problem of planetary proportions.

But the problem, and the search for its solution, is being played out, for better or worse, in the Balkans. Volf says that Jesus once told a cautionary tale about a man with an unclean spirit, that is driven out when the man decides to clean up his act, only to return to the empty space, which has not been filled with compassion, with seven other spirits that are worse than the first; so that 'the final condition of the man is worse than the first.' (Matthew 12:43-45) He says this is the story of the Balkans today. They have tried to clean things up, but only managed to make things worse, much worse, than they were before they started.

Volf says the core issue is that most people have not yet found a way of being able to deal with 'otherness'—other cultures, other traditions, and other religions—apart from seeing it as a 'mess', and trying to 'clean' it up. He says that in this regard, religion which is meant to make things better, often has made things even worse. The Croatian Catholics, Serbian Orthodox, and Bosnian Muslims and Jews, all have different views about what it means to 'clean' up the 'mess'.

Volf says that to embrace the way of Christ is not a way to exclude others. Quite the contrary: to embrace the way of Christ is a way of embracing others, a way of including those that are usually excluded. 'The filth' we need to clean up, Volf says, is not 'others'—other cultures, traditions, and religions—but 'the sin of our own monochrome identity, which is nothing but the sin of exclusion.'[47] This is what Christ himself denounced so unequivocally to Peter.

Volf says 'a refusal to embrace the other, in her otherness, and a desire to purge her from one's world by ostracism or oppression, deportation or liquidation, is ... an exclusion of God[48], 'for our God is a God who loves strangers!'[49]

He reports some as saying that 'too much blood has been shed for us to live together.' But Christ calls us to embrace the other, because the 'only way to peace is through embrace.'[50] An embrace always involves 'a double movement of *aperture* and *closure*.'

> I open my arms to create space in myself for the other. The open arms are a sign of discontent at being myself only, and of a desire to include the other. They are an invitation to the other to come in and feel at home with me, to belong to me. 'In an embrace I close my arms around the other – not tightly, so as to crush her, or assimilate her forcefully into myself; but gently, so as to tell her that I do not want to be without her in her otherness.

'An embrace' Volf says, 'is a *sacrament* of a catholic personality. It mediates the interiority of the other in me, and my complex identity that includes the other, a unity [in diversity].[51] 'It is a microcosm of the new creation [Christ envisaged]'.[52]

In Sarajevo, at the centre of the Balkan conflict, there have been some beautiful living, breathing, all-embracing examples of this new creation. One example is the market. Half a block from the market is the Croatian Catholic cathedral. Just up the street is the Serbian Orthodox church. A few metres away are a historic Muslim mosque and Jewish synagogue.

Sarajevans from each of these religious backgrounds that constitute Bosnia, gather regularly in the market The underlying meaning of the market is the vision of Sarajevo: the commitment of Catholics, Orthodox Muslims and Jews, and other Bosnians, to live together as a single people.

Which is why, on Saturday, 5 February 1994, those opposed to a united multicultural Bosnia blew up the market.

'Those who died in the market', says Jim Douglass, 'are martyrs to a vision of living together. Their blood, that I saw, I saw as the blood of Christ.'[53] But nobody showed the love of Christ more than some anonymous Orthodox neighbours who saved their Muslim friends. In Grbavica, a neighbourhood on the outskirts of Sarajevo, in Serb-held territory that had been systematically 'cleansed', Kruno and Rabija Oprhal, and their son Alen and daughter Irma, survived some of the worst atrocities of the war, because of the compassion of their Serb neighbours.

From the earliest days of the 'cleansing', in April 1992, through to their resettlement in April 1996, their neighbours hid them, kept them safe, and foraged for supplies for them. They recall one of them saying, 'While I am here no one can touch my neighbours!'

Kruno says of his neighbours, 'They were nice. They were kind.' He adds that it was as if, through them, 'God created the situation in which we lived.'[54]

Christ calls us to be a network of residents working towards community in the localities where we live, so as to realise the love of God for all people, particularly those on the fringes of our society.

Christ himself is our example, and his spirit serves as the inspiration for the simple, practical, compassionate path he wants us to take, regardless of the difficulties we may encounter along the way.

His expectation is that we would not slavishly copy him, but voluntarily make the same kind of choices that he made, and that he encouraged his disciples, like Peter, to make: to accept life, to respect life, and to empower people to live life to the full.

Christ calls us to know God, the source of all life, more fully, and to cultivate the disciplines that will help us develop a relationship to God in the midst of our ordinary everyday lives.

He calls us to live in sympathy with the heart of God, sustaining ourselves, supporting one another, and serving those around about us, in an increasingly steadfast, faithful, and life-affirming manner.

Christ calls us to be aware of ourselves, and the gift of life, that each of us can bring to the community.

He calls us to recognise not only the reality of our weaknesses, but also the reality of our strengths, and our responsibility to grow individually as people, in our capacity for self care, self control, and self sacrifice, for the sake of the community.

Christ calls us to be aware of one another, and the gift of life, that every one else can bring to the community.

He calls us to acknowledge not only the reality of our brokenness, but also the potential for wholeness in our relationships, and our responsibility to grow collectively as people, in our capacity to speak truthfully, listen attentively, and work co-operatively, for the sake of the community.

Christ calls us, over and over again, particularly to remember those people in the community who are forgotten, who are rejected, neglected and ignored.

He calls us to affirm our commitment to the welfare of the whole of the human family, and to make ourselves available to brothers and sisters who are marginalised, in their ongoing struggle for love and justice.

Christ knows we disagree about many things, if not most things, but he wants us to agree at least on one thing: the need for us to join together to develop communities in our localities that reflect his compassion by being more devoted, more inclusive, and more non-violent.[55]

Christi-Anarchy

170

Epilogue

The Waiters' Union

In the midst of the hustle and bustle of inner-city Brisbane there is a group of us who feel called to stop, to look, to listen, and, above all, to wait. We want to wait on God, be aware of his presence, attentive to his purpose, and enter into his response to our area. We want to wait on our neighbours: not setting any agendas or setting up any agencies, just helping out in any we way we can.

We have a dream. We dream of a world in which all the resources of the earth will be shared equally between all the people of the earth, so that even the most disadvantaged among us will be able to meet basic needs with dignity and joy. We dream of a great society of small communities cooperating interdependently to practise personal, social, economic and political compassion, love and justice, and peace.

We dream of people developing networks of friendships in which the pain we carry deep down can be shared openly in an atmosphere of mutual support and respect. We dream of people understanding the difficulties we have in common, discussing our problems, discussing the solutions, and working together for personal growth and social change in the light of the love of Christ.

We yearn to make this dream a reality in our own locality. Our locality includes West End, Hill End, Highgate Hill and South Brisbane, tucked into a bend of the Brisbane River. Though it is only twenty minutes walk from Brisbane's city centre, there is very little through traffic. So our area has been able to develop a unique urban village identity, against the background of the general suburban sprawl.

West End has a pretty stable population of about 15,000 people. Even though many of these are transients, there is a very large percentage of older, long-term residents, so the traditions in the neighbourhood are very well established. In the middle of West End is Musgrave Park. In times gone by, the river flats were known for their abundant food, so the Aboriginal inhabitants used the park as a ritual meeting place for tribal celebrations.

The arrival of successive waves of migrants from Mediterranean Europe, Latin America and Indo-China at the South Brisbane railway station, and the availability of the greatest stock of cheap rental accommodation in Queensland, meant that West End became a thriving cosmopolitan centre.

Once you step on to Boundary Street, which runs through the heart of West End, you can feel the casual communitarian atmosphere which characterises the area. It's in the anarchic crowds wandering up and down the road, and in the animated conversations breaking out of the coffee shops and bursting onto the sidewalks.

However, you don't have to look far to realise all is not well in West End. Many people live below the poverty line. And over half the population lives in rented accommodation, the price of which is continually escalating beyond their means to pay. We also have the highest rate of robbery, the second highest rate of car theft, the third highest rate of break-and-entry offences, and the fourth highest rate of sexual offences. And we have the highest rate of violent crime in the state, including murder, attempted murder, conspiracy to murder and manslaughter.

The Waiters' Union consists of some thirty or so households out of the six thousand or so in West End. We do not see ourselves *apart from* the locality. We see ourselves as *a part of* the locality. In fact, we would see ourselves as a network of residents, working towards community in our locality, in the light of the love of Christ for all people, particularly those that are marginalised and disadvantaged.

The Waiters are not a high profile up-front evangelistic group like YWAM. As waiters, keeping a low profile, and working in the background, we simply seek to live in the light of the love of Christ, and do justice to the people in the inner city of Brisbane, for whom the love of Christ ought to be good news.

In order to give ourselves the best chance of faithfully reflecting the love *of* Christ, we seek to develop our relationship *to* Christ, and our relationship to people, *through* Christ.

I find the best way for me to develop my relationship *to* Christ is by encountering him imaginatively as he presents himself in the context of the scriptures. For instance, I may join the man with the withered hand in the synagogue. Sitting beside him I may sense the discomfort he feels about his disability. When Jesus turns to him I see the look of compassion he has in his eyes. When Jesus calls him, I hear the tone of tenderness he has in his voice. I feel the reluctance my neighbour feels in responding to Jesus. Yet I also feel his joy, as he stretches out the withered hand, just as he always wanted to and, to his amazement, his hand is made whole. I share in his excitement at the miracle of healing. And my enthusiasm for this miracle working, working-class Messiah, called Christ, who can make dreams come true, is renewed.

I find the best way for me to develop my relationship *through* Christ is by encountering him imaginatively as he presents himself in the context of my situation. For instance, I may go on an outing with some friends from my area who are quite disadvantaged and do not get out much. We may be cooking some sausages on a barbecue, when I imagine Jesus walking across the park towards us. I imagine Jesus greeting us by name, stopping to spend some time with each of us, paying special attention to each one of us in turn. When he comes to me, I imagine he inquires how I am doing with my friends. He encourages me by saying that he is pleased with how respectful I am. But he also challenges me by telling me to consider how patronising I can be. We talk about some ways I can treat my friends more compassionately. Then, with a smile, he waves goodbye, and walks on. And I am left with a better feel for Christ's dream for my friends and for how I can make Christ's dream for my friends come true.

I personally believe we need to relate to every one through Christ. If we relate to anyone *directly*, the likelihood is that we will react carelessly. When confronted with the plight of the poor, for example, most of us feel overwhelmed by anger or guilt. Without due care, our anger can turn into depression, and our guilt can turn into despair. We can be totally debilitated by an unmediated reaction.

If we relate to everyone *indirectly* through Christ, the likelihood is that we will be able to respond more carefully. When confronted with the plight of the poor, for example, we can use our anger and analyse our guilt constructively. By processing our response through Christ, we can use our outrage to energise our struggle, and we can use our recognition of our wrongs to set things right.

I have found it helpful to approach everyone with a prayer on my lips:

Jesus, Saviour,
may I know your love
and make it known.'

The name of Jesus reminds me of the presence of Christ's love. The notion of 'Saviour' reminds me of the power of Christ's love. And the mantra, 'May I know your love, and make it known,' reminds me of my responsibility, not only to experience Christ's love but also to express Christ's love for all, more faithfully.

Christ's love is for all, I remind myself; not only for those in the community who agree with me, but also for those who don't. We can only share Christ's love through a form that demonstrates the *acceptance* that Jesus extends to all people, regardless of whether they agree with us or not.

This is very difficult for us, because many of us confuse *acceptance* with *agreement*. On the one hand, the more fundamental among us who do not want to give the impression that we agree with everything others do, tend not to accept them. On the other hand, the more liberal among us, who do not want to give the impression that we do not accept others, tend to agree with everything they do.

But Jesus communicated acceptance of those he disagreed with (Luke 7:36-50) and disagreed with those whom he accepted (Luke 9:46-50). For Jesus, acceptance and agreement were not synonymous. The acceptance he extended towards others was not on the basis of agreement with them.

So as people who take Christ seriously, we felt we needed to find a way of demonstrating acceptance regardless of whether we agree with people or not. We found the best way for us to do this was by moving the Waiters from being a *closed set* to being an *open set*. When we act as a closed set the Waiters act as a group of people who agree with certain precepts about Christianity, and only accept as part of our group, other people who agree with the same set of precepts about Christianity. But when we act as an open set, the Waiters act as people who want to develop a relationship with Christ, and help as many other people as we can to develop a relationship with Christ, regardless of whether or not they agree with a certain set of precepts about Christianity.

For us, being an open set has been very scary. Discounting Christianity as a religion has often felt like denying the significance of Christ himself. But Ange and I have persisted, in spite of our anxieties, because we really believe that Christi-Anarchy is essentially not a philosophy about Christ, but a friendship with Christ, and our task as friends of Christ is not to introduce people to a philosophy about Christ, but a friendship with Christ.

A recent survey in Australia indicated that Christians are not significantly different from non-Christians.[1] In fact, we differ only on a few counts, one of which is our attitude towards homosexuality. For most of us, being a Christian means being heterosexual; so for many Christians, to accept homosexuals is an anathema. But, we believe Jesus calls us to demonstrate the same acceptance towards homosexuals as we would towards heterosexuals.

That does not mean we agree with everything homosexuals do, any more than we agree with everything heterosexuals do. But it does mean that we should treat them as respectfully as we treat everybody else. For us, this has involved challenging prejudice in the church, campaigning for non-discrimination in the courts, and welcoming gays and lesbians into our community.

Some time back a young woman, whom we'll call Lyn, came to talk to us about working with us. She'd been informed that we were involved in some innovative community work she was interested in. As we chatted it became obvious that she was quite nervous. I asked her whether there was anything about the way we operated that might be a worry for her.

'I was told you're Christians.' she said.

'Not all of us. But most of us,' I said.

'Well, that could be a problem. Because you're a Christian, and I am a lesbian. And, in my experience,' she said 'Christians and lesbians don't mix.'

'In my experience Christians and lesbians don't mix either,' I said. 'But I am prepared to work on my prejudice if you're prepared to work on yours.'

She smiled, and said she was willing to give it a try. So Lyn came to work with us for a while.

A few months later I had a cup of tea with her, just to check up on how things were going. I asked her whether 'the Christians' were giving her a hard time.

She assured me we were not. Even though she knew we did not necessarily *agree* with lesbian propaganda, she felt we *accepted* her, as a lesbian, in her own right.

Then, suddenly, in the middle of the conversation, Lyn threw back her head, and laughed long and hard.

'You know the funny thing is,' she said; 'it isn't the Christians that are giving me a hard time for being a lesbian. It's the lesbians that are giving me a hard time for hanging around you Christians!'

Christ's love is for all, I remind myself; not only for those in the community who appreciate me, but also for those who don't. So we need to share Christ's love through a stance which demonstrates the *redemption* Jesus extends to all people, regardless of whether they appreciate us or not.

Now this is actually very difficult for us, because many of us seek recognition. Yet we may need to shun recognition, to work anonymously, without any appreciation at all, to do any good in the community.

Jesus did not seek recognition. He entered his neighbourhood incognito (Phil. 2:5-8). Jesus sought redemption rather than recognition. Making time for others, taking on the role of a servant, he went about doing good (Matt. 20:25-28). As those who take Christ seriously we felt we needed to find a way of demonstrating redemption, regardless of whether people appreciate it or not.

We found the best way for us to do this was by moving from acting with a *dispassionate* stance to acting with a *compassionate* stance. When we act with a dispassionate stance, the Waiters interact with the locality as little as we can, in an attempt to keep ourselves, as Christians, 'pure, spotless and unsullied by the world'. But when we act with a compassionate stance the Waiters interact with the locality as much as we can, in the hope that, by rolling up our sleeves, lending a helping hand, and even getting dirt under our fingernails, we may be able to do our bit, as Christ calls us to, to make the world a better place for everybody, Christian and non-Christian alike.

For us, acting with a compassionate stance has been very scary. So much of our self-image as Christians has been vested in keeping ourselves pure, spotless and unsullied. Rolling up sleeves, lending a hand, and getting dirt under our fingernails, to do our bit to make the world a better place for everybody, Christian and non-Christian alike, may be distinctively Christ-like, but it is not definitively Christ-ian.

But Ange and I have persisted, in spite of our anxieties, because we believe Christi-anarchy is essentially not about being Christ-ian, but being Christ-like, and our task as those who want to be like Christ, is to seek to serve the locality as freely, as fully, and as sacrificially, as Christ himself did.

A recent survey in Australia indicated that Christians are among the most unwelcome of any neighbours in any given neighbourhood[2], more than twice as unwelcome as the gays and lesbians that so many of them despise. Apparently, it is because Christians tend to be more dogmatic and more judgmental, and less likely to support despised minority groups.

However, we believe Jesus calls us to demonstrate his *redemption* to everybody, particularly despised minority groups. So we seek to advocate respect for the aspirations of the Aborigines who are the original inhabitants of our area. We seek to help migrants, by learning their language, and teaching them more of our own. We seek to help refugees, by listening to their anguish, and talking over with them about how we can assist in their resettlement. We seek to overcome our handicaps in relating to people with disabilities, by recognising that beneath the differences, we are all the same, and by joining them in a common struggle to love and to be loved. And we seek to respond to the pain of battered women, broken men, and abused kids, by protecting them from the threat of violence, and by supporting them in their quest for justice.

But we have no illusions about Christ's redemptive work beginning or ending with us. Christians don't have a monopoly on Christ, and we don't have a franchise on Christ's redemptive work in the community. However, we are all called—Christian and non-Christian alike—to recognise Christ's redemption at work in the community and to co-operate with it the best that we can.

The other night, a loud fight broke out next door. Living in an inner city area with a high crime rate, it seems that there is always someone breaking in or a fight breaking out somewhere in our area. Thefts do not annoy me that much, at least not when robbery is without violence. Thieves can be in and out of your house before you know it. In fact, I actually slept right through the last time our place was burgled. But fights really annoy me. Brutality always involves violence. And violence means somebody is going to get hurt, sometimes get hurt very badly. It was not very long ago that, in a domestic dispute that erupted at our local fish and chip shop, a man shot his ex-wife in the face and wounded two of her friends who tried to protect her.

So when the fight broke out next door, I immediately felt my heart begin to pound, impelling me to intervene before our elderly neighbours became the next casualties in our neighbourhood. However, before I could move, my neighbour Ronnie sprang into action. Ronnie called out to the angry young man next door, whom we will call Leon, and who he suspected might be beating up his elderly parents.

'Leon, Leon!' Ronnie cried. 'What's going on in there? Tell me what's going on in there!' But there was no reply, only the pathetic sound of crashing and screaming, as if bodies were being knocked about the place.

So Ronnie rushed out and round to the neighbour's house where he started banging on the front door, demanding some kind of response. 'Leon!' Ronnie cried. 'Come here! I want to speak with you! Come on now!' Again there was no reply. But soon the sounds inside the house began to subside, and somebody opened the door.

As soon as the door opened, Ronnie walked straight in. Leon was hurling his fists about to prevent anyone from interfering in the fight, but Ronnie calmly strode up to Leon, put his arm around his shoulders, and carefully ushered him out of the house.

After Ronnie had taken Leon round the block a few times, he brought him over to join us on the veranda. While I spoke with Leon, Ange, my wife, went over to speak with Leon's mum and dad, about what could be done about his abusive behaviour in future.

As I sat there sipping my cup of tea, sharing a plate of biscuits with Leon, I reflected on the events of the evening. It certainly had not turned out as I had expected it would. It was far more traumatic than I had imagined it would be. But it was also far more beautiful than I had imagined it would be.

Ronnie, who is by his own admission anything but religious, had demonstrated redemption, right there and then, in our midst. He had assumed responsibility for the welfare of his neighbours. He had not projected the responsibility to help on to anyone else. He had understood, in a crisis, responsibility always requires action. He had not prevaricated. He had acted promptly and appropriately. He had also taken a great risk of getting beaten up in the process. As a result of his Christ-like action, Ronnie had saved Leon from doing great damage to his parents, and Leon's mum and dad had been saved from having to struggle on their own with the psychotic rage of their son.

For us, the love of Christ is at the heart of each and every situation that we encounter. And, for us, to solve problems inherent in each and every situation, depends on people being able to feel something of the love of Christ for themselves and for others, and so to be free to transcend their anger and guilt and inadequacy, and to act in a beautiful, Christ-like, radical, sacrificial compassionate manner. However, because of their experience of Christianity, most of the people we work with are not only non-Christian, but also quite anti-Christian. So the challenge for us is to try to introduce them to the Christ of Christi-anarchy—as opposed to Christianity—without alienating them any more than they already are.

Ange and I do this through practising a simple, centred, problem-solving process. We agree to work with people, struggling with the issues that are important to them, on the basis of *common sense* and *consensus*. Because Ange and I believe Christ is the source of all truth, and the truth is written, as the scripture says, on the hearts of all people, we believe that Christ's truth is often expressed in the common sense that people speak, sometimes without their even knowing it. We dialogue with people about their problems and about possible solutions to their problems, and try to decide on a particular course of action that we can take together.

Quite often, to the embarrassment of Christians, who claim to have an exclusive right to the truth, it is those who do not make any such claims who seem to be more intuitively in touch with the reality of their problems, and the reality of possible solutions.

Ange and I will only decide on taking a particular course of action if we are personally convinced that it will move us in a direction that is true to the *compassion* of Christ, and demonstrates his *acceptance* and his *redemption,* in relation to the resolution of the problem. However, Ange and I can usually, if not invariably, come to a consensus with sensible people over the way they want to go about solving their problems. This is because—whether they know it or not—there is no fundamental conflict between this and the way Christ want us to go about solving our problems.

Neither want unethical shortcuts. Both want genuine, loving, just, long-term, sustainable solutions. Sometimes the connection between the way that we have chosen to go, and the way of Christ, remains *implicit*. But sometimes it becomes *explicit*.

I love to tell people who are celebrating a successful resolution of a problem, that, without them knowing, their success is a result of their having taken the way of Christ. Regardless of their attitude to Christ, they cannot deny the successful resolution of the problem, or disregard the value of the way of Christ they have taken thus far.

As a result, the way of Christ becomes a significant *point of view*. Some see it as one point of view among many. But some start to see it as the one point of view by which the many may be judged. Thus the way of Christ becomes a significant *point of reference*. If people adopt the way of Christ as the point of reference for decision-making in their everyday lives, then the process of conversion to Christ as a person, not Christianity as a religion, has begun, and our dream of personal growth and social change in the light of the love of Christ is coming true.

Some time back, the landlords in our neighbourhood went into a frenzy of jacking up their rents. The vulnerable people in our locality, who were dependent on the availability of cheap rental accommodation for their survival, were beside themselves with worry. A number of community meetings were called to come up with a plan to solve the problem.

One suggestion was guerrilla warfare led by chainsaw-wielding storm troopers, who would cut the power brokers off at the knees! The idea brought about an avalanche of applause. But after it was over, everyone acknowledged the prospect was repugnant.

I sat there trying to think of an approach that would be acceptable both to Christ and the community. Eventually an idea came to me, and I got to my feet and strode to the front of the meeting.

'I feel I need to go on a hunger strike. To fight against the greed that's wrecking our community. And to fight for the rights of everyone in our community, whether they are rich or poor, to have affordable access to secure tenancy.' People clapped. So I continued to speak.

'I'm not going to break my fast until fifty landlords promise not to increase their rents by more than ten per cent, fifty tenants promise to support responsible landlords and expose irresponsible landlords, and fifty residents promise to help landlords and tenants negotiate a just settlement of this dispute by publicly commending those who do and publicly condemning those who don't!'

People cheered. So the plan was carried.

After the meeting a young man called Steve Haynes came up to us and spoke to us about the plan. Steve said he liked the plan because it was active, it addressed the issues for all the parties in the dispute, and it called upon the factions in our community to fight together for a common cause.

We said we would be glad if Steve could join us in putting the plan into action. So Steve signed on for the campaign.

Each day a few people would join me on my hunger strike in Boundary Street, collecting signatures of landlords, tenants and residents who promised to help us to solve the rental problem in West End. One landlord agreed not to raise his rents at all. Another landlord, responding to an appeal by his tenants over the matter of a raise in rent imposed by a real estate agent, fired the real estate agent and fixed the rent back at the original rate. Yet another owner, upon discovering that his tenants were going through a tough time financially, actually reduced the rent tor a period of time.

All these landlords were presented with bunches of flowers to commend them for their sense of responsibility. The presentations took place on national television to encourage them, and others like them, to continue to act as responsible citizens in our community.

Steve was amazed that we had been able to get so many landlords on our side, and was amused with our tactics for keeping them there. We talked with Steve about how the line dividing good and evil runs not between classes, such as landlords and tenants; but right down the middle of every individual: landlords, tenants, the residents – everyone. We talked about the potential that all of us, landlords as well as tenants, have to respond to the challenge to renounce evil and embrace good.

However, not everybody responded well to the challenge of renouncing the evil of capitalism and embracing the good of the community. One landlord in particular proved to be totally ruthless in his pursuit of a profit. Apparently, he beat up his tenant, a woman by the name of Kimberly Williams, who could not pay the inordinate rent he demanded; then, he literally threw her down the stairs, in his haste to get her out of his flat as fast as he could.

Ange and I went to talk with Kimberly. We listened to the story and were convinced of its veracity. We assured her of our support, and became firm friends.

Ange and I then went to talk with the landlord. He was not interested at all in anything we had to say. He told us he had the right to run his business in any way he wanted. We tried to suggest that he had the right to run his business any way he wanted to as long as he did not infringe the rights of others to safety and security. He told us we had no right to call him to account since he was only accountable to himself, his family and his bank balance. When we challenged that, he told us to get out, and threatened to kill us if we ever came back. As far as he was concerned, we had become mortal enemies.

Because we were afraid, we felt like backing off. But we felt constrained to be faithful to the cause, in spite of the death threat hanging over our heads. So we organised a group of residents, to camp on the door step of the recalcitrant landlord, to bring home to him the reality of the homelessness that his callousness was causing. While we were there, we discussed the issues with the landlord, his family, and his neighbours. But while some of his neighbours were very supportive, and some of his family were very sympathetic, the landlord was totally unwilling to negotiate.

Eventually we took him to court on a charge of the assault he had committed against Kimberly. When he was found guilty we requested the judge to give him six months community work with us as a sentence, in the hope that we could sort things out by serving the community together. The landlord never did figure us out, and was furious with us till the day he died.

After nine days we had the backing of fifty landlords who promised not to increase their rents by more than ten per cent, fifty tenants who would support responsible landlords and expose irresponsible landlords, and fifty residents who would help landlords and tenants negotiate a just settlement of the dispute.

These people not only did a great deal themselves, but also put pressure on various levels of government to do a lot more. We were therefore able to organise a series of community consultations that became the most comprehensive process in town planning the Brisbane City Council had ever engaged in. As a result, affordable accommodation was put back on the agenda for our area. So on the tenth day, we broke our fast with doner kebabs at a local Lebanese restaurant.

Kimberly, the tenant, on whose behalf we had fought the landlord who beat her up and threatened to kill us, came to believe in us through the part we had played. In fact, Jim and Anne took Kimberly into their home, where she stayed, on and off, for years, till she got a housing commission flat of her own. During the time she stayed with them, Jim and Anne shared with Kimberly the faith in Christ that sustains their 'amazing' lifestyle. And though she says she'll never share their 'crazy' lifestyle, Kimberly has come to share Jim and Anne's faith in Christ.

Steve, who had joined our campaign, was intrigued with the way we had tried to manage the conflict as constructively as we could. We had checked out the facts. We had chatted with the landlord and the tenant face to face. We had confronted the landlord clearly and cogently, calling him to account for his actions. We had cared for the tenant simply and practically; helping her with alternative accommodation. And we had seen the conflict through to a resolution, in spite of the death threats; being as respectful as we possibly could in the process.

'That's a great way to go,' said Steve. 'It's a really creative way to approach conflict resolutions. Where did you guys get the idea from?'

'You really want to know?' we asked.

'Yeah, seriously, I really want to know.' he said.

'Christ.' we said.

'Christ?' he asked in disbelief.

'Yeah' we answered. 'You may find it difficult to believe. But the way we have been trying to deal with things round here, is just the way Christ taught people to do it!'

'That's incredible!' he said. 'Most of the Christians I know aren't even interested in housing issues; let alone in dealing with housing disputes through direct action.'

Apparently Steve had been brought up as a Catholic. He'd gone to mass regularly with his Mum, and at one time he'd been quite devout. But he'd decided to chuck it all in, he said, because 'they were so conservative' - and had no answers to the bigger questions he'd been asking about global justice.

'Well,' we said, 'if you read the gospels you'll find that Christ was not only very committed to the poor, and the issues that impacted on the poor, but he was also prepared to take action, even direct action, to stand with the poor against those who oppressed them.'

'Is that so?' he asked.

'It is!' we answered.

So Steve went off, with renewed resolve, to scrap everything he'd learnt about Christianity thus far, and to get properly acquainted with the Christ that strode through the pages of the gospels.

A little later we met up with Steve again. He said he'd read the gospels, and was so impressed with the person he'd encountered in the scriptures, that he'd begun to look to Christ as a guide for making some major decisions about the way he wanted to live his life. Steve began to get together with a bloke by the name of Peter Westoby, who was a member of the Waiters' Union at the time, and with Peter's support he began to make some big changes in his life.

Steve had been troubled by bouts of psychotic depression, that were aggravated by doing dope, and Peter stuck by him through his periods of distress. Eventually, Steve decided it was time to give up the dope. He started to cultivate a sustainable rhythm of work and rest, which maximised his creativity, minimised his stress, and helped him manage his own mental and emotional health a whole lot better. Then he got involved as an organiser, with Grow, a peer counselling group, helping other people with a range of physical and psychiatric disabilities make the most of their lives.

At the same time as all this was happening, Steve was getting to know the Catholic Workers. For Steve, getting to know Jim and Ann was like coming home. They were Catholic, but unlike any other Catholics Steve had met before; they were anarchists, just like him. The Catholic Workers, with their radical response to global issues, were just the kind of people Steve said he had been looking for all his life.

With their encouragement, Steve and his partner Judy managed to develop a way of life that has become the envy of all the anarchists I know. With their two children, Julia and Christopher, Steve and Judy live in secure tenant-managed accommodation, owned by the housing co-operative of which they are a part; and Steve has developed his own self-managed employment programme, a carpentry business, building beautiful furniture, and restoring old houses. Steve and Judy also play a vital part in sustaining the ethos of the Waiters' Union; not only taking their own initiatives, but also supporting the initiatives that other people in the network take towards community development in the neighbourhood.

Steve is involved in helping with a Boarding House Project, which provides affordable housing for people who are disadvantaged. And Judy is involved in helping at the Bristol Street Household, which provides hospitality, company and emergency accommodation for people who are in distress.

Steve and Judy Collins-Haynes show us Christi-Anarchy at work, as they, with Christ, seek to build a better world: not just for themselves, but for everybody, out of the ruins of their broken dreams.

Christi-Anarchy /kristiaeneki/ *n.* Christlike life; lifestyle characterised by the radical non-violent sacrificial compassion of Jesus the Christ; way of life distinguished by commitment to love and to justice; working from the bottom up to empower people, particularly the marginalised and disadvantaged, so as to enable them to realise their potential, as men and women, made in the image of God, through self-directed, other-orientated intentional community groups and organisations; from '*Christi*'-'**for Christ**', and '*anarche*'-'**against the powers**', as in '**the principalities and powers**'.

Notes

Section One

1   H Ellerbe, *The Dark Side Of Christian History*, Morningstar Books, San Rafael, 1995

2   JN Higarth, *The Conversion Of Western Europe*, Prentice Hall, Englewood Cliffs, 1969, p. 49

3   CM Smith, *The Pearly Gates Syndicate,* Doubleday, New York, 1971, p. 27

4   Smith, *The Pearly Gates Syndicate,* p. 28

5   W Nigg, *The Heretics: Heresy Through The Ages*, Dorset Press, New York, 1962, p. 127

6   Higarth, p. 46

7   JH Smith, *The Death Of Classical Paganism*, Charles Scribner, New York, 1976, p. 49

8   Ellerbe, p. 29

9   HW Robinson, *Christian Doctrine Of Man*, T & T Clark, Edinburgh, 1926, p. 180

10   EH Broadbent, *The Pilgrim Church*, Pickering & Inglis, London, 1974, p. 27

11   E Pagels, *Adam, Eve and the Serpent*, Random House, New York, 1988, p. 125

12   Ellerbe, p. 28

13   L Graham, *Deceptions and Myths of the Bible*, Citadel Press, New York, 1975, p. 444

14   Ellerbe, p. 41

15   C Panati, *Panati's Extraordinary Endings of Practically Everything*, Harper & Row, New York, 1989, pp. 225-228

16   Panati, pp. 225-228

17   Panati, pp. 225-228

18   Ellerbe, p. 62

19   Ellerbe, p. 52

20   P Schaff, *History Of The Christian Church* Vol V, Wm.B.Eerdmans, Grand Rapids, 1952, p. 75-76

21   JB Russell, *A History of Medieval Christianity*, Thomas Y. Cromwell, New York, 1968, p. 92

22   Russell, p. 92

23   Broadbent, p. 57

24   Broadbent, p. 43

25   Broadbent, p. 49

26   Broadbent, p. 53

27   Broadbent, pp. 53-54

28   Broadbent, p. 52

29   Broadbent, p. 53

30   Ellerbe, p. 59

31   Ellerbe, p. 62

32   Ellerbe, p. 62

33   ·H Daniel-Rops, *Cathedral And Crusade*, E.P. Dutton & Co., New York, 1957, p. 241

34   Ellerbe, p. 64

35   Daniel-Rops, p. 276

36   Ellerbe, p. 68

37   Daniel-Rops, pp. 439-441

38   JB Russell, *A History of Medieval Christianity*, pp. 159-160

39   Ellerbe, p. 65

40   M Martin, *Decline and Fall of the Roman Church*, GP Putnam's Sons, New York, 1981, p. 134

41   JA Haught, *Holy Horrors*, Prometheus, Buffalo, 1990 , pp. 25-26

42   H Daniel-Rops, p. 547

43   HC Lea, *The Inquisition Of The Middle Ages*, MacMillan, New York, 1961, p. 177

44 Lea, p. 174

45 RH Robbins, *The Encyclopaedia of Witchcraft and Demonology*, Bonanza Books, New York, 1981, p. 13

46 Lea, p. 214

47 J Plaidy, *The Spanish Inquisition*, Citadel Press, New York, 1967, p. 139

48 Ellerbe, p. 83

49 GG Coulton, *Inquisition and Liberty*, Peter Smith, Glouster, 1969, p. 155

50 Ellerbe, p. 83

51 Ellerbe, pp. 81-82

52 Ellerbe, p. 82

53 Lea, pp. 233-236

54 Nigg, p. 220

55 P Tompkins, 'Symbols of Heresy' in *The Magic Of Obelisks*, Harper, New York, 1981, p. 57

56 KS Latourette, *A History Of Christianity*, Harper & Row, Vol.II New York, 1975, p. 689ff

57 Latourette, p. 923

58 Latourette, p. 924

59 R Stupperich, 'Martin Luther' in *The History Of Christianity*, Lion Publishing, Berkhamstead, 1977, p. 363

60 A Lindt, 'John Calvin' in *The History Of Christianity*, Lion Publishing, Berkhamstead, 1977, p. 381

61 A Kreider & JH Yoder, 'Christians And War' in *The History Of Christianity*, Lion Publishing, Berkhamstead, 1977, p. 24

62 HA Mulligan, 'Columbus Saga Sinking Fast', Associated Press, 8 March 1992

63 *World Book*, Vol IV, World Book Encyclopaedia Inc, Sydney, 1995, p. 210

64 *World Book*, Vol IV, p. 368

65 S Neill, *A History Of Christian Missions*, Penguin Books, Harmondsworth, 1975, p. 169

66 *World Book*, Vol XV, p. 530

67 Latourette, Vol.II, p. 944ff

68 Plaidy, p. 165

69 Latourette, p. 944ff

70 Neill, p. 171

71 C Roth, *The Spanish Inquisition*, WW Norton & Co., New York, 1964, p. 221

72 R Barraclough, *Land Rights*, Student Christian Movement, Brisbane, 1988, pp. 2-3

73 Russell, p. 173

74 Nigg, p. 281

75 BG Walker, *The Woman's Dictionary of Myths and Secrets*, Harper & Row, San Francisco, 1969, p. 1004

76 K Thomas, *Religion and the Decline of Magic*, Charles Scribner's Sons, 1974, p. 278

77 Ellerbe, p. 127

78 BP Levack, *The Witch-Hunt in Early Modern Europe*, Longman, London, 1987, p. 105

79 H Kamen, *Inquisition and Society in Spain*, Indiana University Press, Bloomington, 1985, p. 164

80 Robbins, p. 3

81 DJ Goldhagen, *Hitler's Willing Executioners*, Abacus, London, 1997, pp. 301-302

82 Goldhagen, pp. 241-242

83 Goldhagen, p. 369

84 Goldhagen, p. 14

85 Goldhagen, p. 43

86 Goldhagen, pp. 49-50

87 Goldhagen, p. 111

88 Goldhagen, p. 110

89 Goldhagen, pp. 108-109, 111

90 Goldhagen, p. 114

91 Goldhagen, p. 114

92 S Diamond, *Spiritual Warfare*, South End Press, Boston, 1989, p. 176

93 Diamond., 176

94 *Living Words* Newsletter, Paralife Ministries, September/October 1986, p. 8

95 Diamond, p. 170

96 Diamond, p. 16-17

97 Diamond, p. 171

98 Diamond, p. 166

99 Diamond, p. 164

100 Diamond, p. 164

101 Diamond, p. 165

102 Diamond, p. 165

103 'You Heard It Right: The Dictator Is An Evangelical Christian', *Christianity Today*, 23 April 1982, p. 33

104 Diamond, p. 165

105 G Black, *Garrison Guatemala*, Zed Books, London, 1984, p. 144

106 Black, p. 144

107 Diamond, p. 166

108 J Collins, 'Rwanda', *Target*, No.4, TEAR Australia, Melbourne, 1994 , p. 16

109 Collins, p. 16

110 J Steward, *Rwanda Report*, Rwanda: Email, 1997, p. 1

111 T Adeyemo, *Lessons From Rwanda*, Lecture, TEAR Australia Conference, 1996

112 Steward, p. 1

113 Steward, p. 1

114 F Wood, *The Arrogance Of Faith*, Alfred A. Knopf, New York, 1990, p. 27

Section Two

1 MS Peck, *The People Of The Lie*, Rider Books, Melbourne, 1983, pp. 69-76

2 H Ellerbe, *The Dark Side Of Christian History*, Morningstar Books, San Rafael, 1995, p. 32

3 Ellerbe, p. 80

4 Ellerbe, p. 80

5 J Margolis, 'War of Words over Columbus rages on', *The Sunday Denver Post*, 28 July 1991, p. 7

6 *World Book*, Vol IV, World Book Encyclopaedia Inc, Sydney, 1995, p. 368

7 J Dominion, *Authority*, Darton, Longman & Todd, London, 1976, p. 11

8 Dominion, p. 12

9 D Andrews, *Building A Better World*,

Albatross, Sutherland, 1996, p. 115

10 B Tuchman, B. *A Distant Mirror*, New York: Ballentine Books, 1978, p. 322

11 E Canetti, *Crowds and Power*, Picador? Penguin?1960, p.

12 K Thomas, *Religion and The Decline Of Magic*, 551

13 M Weber, *The Theory Of Social And Economic Organisations*, Glencoe: Free Press, 1947

14 S Diamond, *Spiritual Warfare*, 15

15 Ibid., 166

16 G Sharp, *Power and Struggle*, Boston: Porter Sargent Publishers, 1973, p. 12

17 H Kamen, *Inquistion and Society in Spain*, 161

18 W Wink, *Engaging the Powers*, Minneapolis: Fotress Press, 1992, pp. 42-43 (adapted)

19 Wink, p. 4

20 F Peretti, *This Present Darkness* and *Piercing The Darkness*, Crossways Books, Westchester, 1988

21 BP Levack, *The Witch-Hunt in Early Modern Europe*, 97

22 Ibid., 97

23 Wink, p. 4

24 Alpert, R. *Be Here Now*, 107

25 Ellerbe,H. *The Dark Side Of Christianity*, 12

26 Wink, p. 5

27 Freud,S. *The Future Of Illusion*, London: Hogarth, 1961, p. 30

28 Marx, K. 'Debates On Freedom Of The Press' *Early Texts*, Oxford: Oxford University Press,, 1971, p. 35

29 Wink, p. 6

30 Kelsey, M. *The Other Side Of Silence*, New York: Paulist Press, 1976, p. 147

31 Wink, p. 6

32 Elliott, C. *Comfortable Compassion*, London: Hodder and Stoughton, 1987, p. 153

33 Latourette,K.S. *A History Of Christianity*,

p. 924

34 M Rokeach, *The Open and Closed Mind*, Basic Books, 1960

35 D Wright, *Psychology and Moral Behaviour*, Penguin 1971

36 S Stouffer, *Communism, Conformity, and Civil Liberties*, Doubleday, 1955

37 J Ellul, *The Ethics of Freedom*, Grand Rapids: Wm. B. Eerdmans, 1967, pp. 88-90

38 P Allport and B Kramer, 'Some Roots of Prejudice', *Journal of Psychology*, 1946, pp. 9–39

39 P Glew-Crouch, *Religion and Helping Behaviour*, Tasmania: University of Tasmania, 1989

40 R Stellaway, 'Religion', *Christian Perspectives of Sociology*, Zondervan, 1982, p. 54

41 Stellaway, p. 255

42 D Andrews, *Working Towards Community In Our Religion*, Kew: Zadok, 1993, p. 4

43 M West, *A View From The Ranges*, HarperCollins, Sydney, 1996, p. 5

44 West, p. 6

45 West, p. 11

46 West, p. 6

47 West, p. 6-7

48 D Hyde, *Rescuing Jesus*, Kew: Mandarin Books, 1997, p. 6

49 Hyde, p. 6

50 Hyde, p. 6

51 Hyde, p. 6-14, 133

52 P Cameron, *Fundamentalism and Freedom*, Doubleday Books, Sydney, 1995, p. 6-7

53 Ibid., 7

54 A Dillard, in A Corn, (Ed) *Incarnation*, Penguin, New York, 1990, p. 36

55 J Ellul, *The Subversion Of Christianity*, Eerdmans, Grand Rapids, 1986, p. 13, 38

56 W Reich, *The Murder Of Christ*, Simon & Schuster, 1953

57 Ellul, *The Subversion Of Christianity*, p. 13

58 Reich, cited in Hyde, adapted

59 Ellul, *The Subversion Of Christianity*, p. 6

60 T Cahill, *How The Irish Saved Civilisation!* Hodder & Stoughton, London, 1995, p. 148

61 A Wilson, *Jesus, The Evidence*, HarperCollins, 1992

62 J Ellul, *The Ethics Of Freedom*, Eerdmans, Grand Rapids, 1976, p. 12, 88-90

63 Ellul, *The Ethics Of Freedom*, p. 50

Section Three

1 W Berry, *Sex, Freedom, & Community*, Pantheon Books, San Francisco, 1992, p. 94

2 Berry, p. 94

3 Berry, p. 96

4 Berry, p. 115

5 A Whitehead, *Process And Reality*, Free Press, 1978

6 J Ellul, *The Subversion Of Christianity*, Eerdmans, Grand Rapids, 1986, p. 11

7 E Peterson, 2 Thessalonians 2: 3-4, *The Message*, NavPress, Colorado Springs, 1993, p. 436

8 P Hiebert, 'Conversion, Culture, and Cognitive Categories', *Gospel In Context*, (Vol.1, No.4, October 1978, pp. 24-29

9 Hiebert, pp. 26-27

10 R Brinsmead, *The Two Sources Of Morality and Religion*, Henry Holt, New York, 1989, pp. 5-7

11 Brinsmead, p. 7

12 S Hauerwas, *After Christendom?* Abingdon Press, Nashville, 1991, pp. 138-140

13 T Todorov, *The Conquest Of America*, Harper Torchbooks, New York, 1987, pp. 168-169

14 Hauerwas, pp. 153-161 (adapted)

15 J Peterson, *Church Without Walls*, New Press, Colorado, 1992, p. 174

16   S Jones, *The Way*, Hodder & Stoughton, London, 1947, p. 59

17   Jones, p. 57

18   Jones, p. 51

19   Jones, p. 52

20   Jones, p. 54

21   Jones, p. 55

22   Jones, p. 55

23   Jones, p. 56

24   A Nolan, *Jesus Before Christianity*, Darton, Longman & Todd, London, 1977, pp. 136-138

25   Brinsmead, p. 111

26   P Palmer, *To Know As We Are Known*, Harper, San Francisco, 1993, p. 49

27   Palmer, pp. 48,49,51

28   D Lama, *The Good Heart*, Rider, London, 1997, p. 83,84

29   M Gandhi, *The Message Of Jesus*, Bharitya Vidya Bhavan, Bombay, 1971, foreword

30   Gandhi, p. 7

31   Gandhi, p. 111

32   Gandhi, afterword

33   Gandhi, p. 40, 79

Section Four

1   D Goleman, *Emotional Intelligence*, Bantam Books, New York, 1995, p. xiv

2   Goleman, pp. 276-277

3   W Wink, *Engaging the Powers*, Minneapolis: Fotress Press, 1992, pp. 17-31

4   Goleman, p. 119

5   Goleman, pp. 328-329

6   J Macmurray, *Freedom In The Modern World*, Faber&Faber, London, 1958, pp. 28-29

7   Macmurray, p. 55

8   Macmurray, pp. 88-90

9   Macmurray, pp. 58-59

10   Macmurray, pp. 65-70

11   S Keen, *Fire In The Belly*, Bantam Books, New York, 1991, p. 102

12   C Jung, 'The Development Of Personality', *Collected Works*, Routledge, Kegan, & Paul, London, 1953, pp. 167-187

13   S Keen, *Fire In The Belly*, pp. 246-268

14   D Richardson, *Eternity In Their Hearts*, Regal Books, Ventura, 1981

15   G Rosendale, 'Maladikarra', *Sunrise Times*, Wontulp Productions, Hermit Park, pp. 1-2

16   Rosendale, p. 2

17   T Jinpa, 'The Buddhist Context', *The Good Heart*, Rider, London, 1997, pp. 169-171

18   D Lama, *The Good Heart*, Rider, London, 1997, p. 83

19   Jinpa, p. 170

20   *Bhagavad Gita*, ch. 4, vv. 6-8

21   M Gandhi, *My Religion*, Navajivan Press, Ahmedabad, 1985, pp. 58-62

22   A Hingorani & G Hingorani, *The Encyclopaedia Of Gandhian Thoughts*, All India Congress Committee, New Delhi, 1985, p. 159

23   Hingorani, pp. 236-237

24   E Easwaren, *A Man To Match His Mountains*, Nilgiri Press, Petaluma, 1984, p. 103

25   Easwaren, p. 63

26   R Kumar, 'Abdul Ghaffar Khan', *Khan Abdul Ghaffar Khan*, p. 215

27   Easwaren, p. 117

28   *The Koran*, Ch. ii v. p. 213

29   *The Koran*, Ch.ii v. p. 109

30   *The Koran*, Ch. ii v. p. 264

31   *The Koran*, Ch.v v. p. 32

32   E Wiesel, *Messengers of God*, Simon & Schuster, New York, 1977, p. 156

33   M Unger, 'Joseph', *The World Book Encyclopedia*, Field Enterprises, Vol.11 Chicago, 1974, p. 133